LIVE
MORE

WANT
LESS

LIVE
MORE

52 WAYS TO **FIND ORDER** IN YOUR LIFE

MARY CARLOMAGNO

WANT
LESS

Storey Publishing

The mission of Storey Publishing is to serve our customers by publishing practical information that encourages personal independence in harmony with the environment.

Edited by Deborah Balmuth and Dale Evva Gelfand
Art direction and cover design by Dan O. Williams
Book design by Nathan Padavick
Illustrations by © Nathan Padavick

Storey Publishing
210 MASS MoCA Way
North Adams, MA 01247
www.storey.com

Printed in the United States by Versa Press
10 9 8 7 6 5 4 3 2 1

Library of Congress Cataloging-in-Publication Data

Carlomagno, Mary.
 Live more, want less / by Mary Carlomagno.
   p. cm.
 Includes index.
 ISBN 978-1-60342-558-2 (pbk. : alk. paper)
 1. Storage in the home. 2. Organization. 3. Orderliness.
 4. Decision making. I. Title.
TX309.C367 2011
648'.8—dc22
                          2010029330

**FOR MATTY,
MY LITTLE SAINT IN THE CITY**

I would like to thank the Storey family
for making room for this city girl's ideas
among all their great country wisdom.
Special thanks to Pam Art for her patience
and commitment, to Deborah Balmuth
for her keen observation skills and vision,
to Dale Evva Gelfand for her eagle-eye
editing, to Dan Reynolds for his endless
enthusiasm, and especially to my longtime
friend and colleague Amy Greeman, who
made this book happen.

Contents

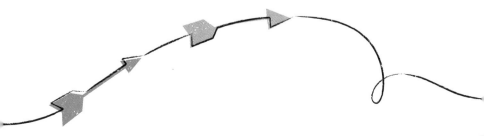

Introduction

IS YOUR LIFE out of order? Are your wants and desires getting in the way of happiness? Would you like to get your life *in* order and find the freedom to live more fully? What, exactly, does getting your life in order mean? Order is not a one-size-fits-all proposition; rather, it's a personalized journey where *you* write the itinerary.

Perhaps you feel that your life is leading you rather than the other way around. Or maybe you reach the end of the day feeling overwhelmed and exhausted instead of fulfilled and contented. Perhaps you are yearning for a deeper understanding of life and have trouble pinpointing exactly where to begin. Even with all our modern conveniences, where technology is at our fingertips and material possessions abound, this quest can seem elusive. But it does not have to be. Just as you customize your iPod or Google job search, you can customize how order takes shape in your life, which begins with stripping away the nonessentials. Call it blank slating: setting the foundation for change, creativity, and even enlightenment.

Some of you may view getting organized, time management, or other such buzzwords as restrictive, impossible-to-manage systems that force an unnatural change — but the opposite is true. When you release, simplify, and clear distractions, you open yourself up to an entirely new kind of freedom, movement, and discovery. This way of thinking is contrary to what most people believe about organizing or clutter clearing, and it's the reason that I was motivated to start a company to answer this need: **order.** It represents a new starting point, one that begins with asking if you really need and use the things you have. After all, anything can be contained, boxed, or stored; just visit the Container Store or Target to see a whole host of beautiful options.

But that is secondary. The first decision is choosing lightness over heaviness; opting to subtract, not add; and finally making choices that free you of distractions so that you can find more meaning in life. This is the basis of my company and the basis of this book, a set of lessons and practices that inform your journey to finding order. And while this plan is structured on a year of lessons — one "WAY" per week — you can pick it up at any point and pull out what is meaningful for you right now. The 52 WAYs are designed for you to re-experience, revisit, and restart each year.

Grouped by true-life examples either from a client or a personal story and then summarized in an overarching theme, each WAY is followed by "Daily Practices" that provide practical actions — ones you can follow every day of the year if you choose. This step-by-step blueprint coaxes subtle shifts in the way you view your things, your relationships, your work, and your passions. It is my belief that these daily practices or rituals inform how we live — and, in turn, how we transform, evolve, and grow. They will provide you with the tools you need to make a change — one that contrary to popular belief does not happen overnight. At least it didn't for me.

By nature, I am extremely organized. I have an innate ability to know where things go. I enjoy rearranging closets, straightening out spice racks, cleaning up kids' clutter, and

updating filing systems. People call me to organize their spaces and, consequently, their lives. They pay me to tell them what to do with their stuff. But what I really do is force people to make decisions that they cannot make on their own. This instinctively comes easy to me. I know where the picnic basket is supposed to go, I can tell why you don't have time to write that novel, and I can see why your credit card bills are too high. I just know; I always have. Organizing projects were plentiful in my family, in which I am the youngest child and only daughter, so organizing has always been a part of my life. My father was a Depression-era saver, my mother is a skilled shopper, and my brother is best known for buying and returning just about everything that Bed Bath & Beyond offers. Organizing is in my blood, so this career comes naturally.

I began organizing professionally seven years ago when shopping — another one of my innate abilities — spiraled out of control. Shopping became more than just a pastime; it was taking up all of my time and most of my money. But my skill at finding the latest trends at bargain prices coupled with my uncanny ability to organize gave me a unique perspective. I ran my home like a good retail store, rotating seasonal merchandise in and out. Once I was done with an item, I donated it, consigned it, or sold it on eBay to free up prime real estate in my closets. (This is still my SOP.) My sorting skills were being honed by virtue of my lifestyle. Who would have thought that all those years of shopping and lunching with my mother would be put to such good use? Shopping converged with organizing to create a career where now I help others. There is comfort in saying to my clients, "I have been there." And by "there" I mean Bloomingdales!

Unlike other home-repair workers — plumbers, electricians, carpenters — whom I have begun to liken myself to, my only tools are my instincts, an undeniable opinion on the right thing to do. I will find out what else is required when I arrive at the job site. Not long ago I was traipsing around the sample sales of Manhattan, purchasing bags of "must have" apparel that would never be worn. Nowadays I don my new uniform of jeans, T-shirt, and loafers. I consider the money I no longer rack up on my American Express bill as a byproduct of my career makeover.

Being an organizer is more than simply sorting and storing possessions; it is a deep dive into a sea of messy problems. Part therapist and part best friend, I piece together the client's life, the series of events that led him or her to the call for help. My questions begin: What does your space look like? When was the last time you tried to get organized? What were the results? Anything I can glean from these initial queries will tell me what I can expect. Most importantly, I am trying to determine the "Big Kahuna" of the call: is this client ready to change? Within a few minutes I can tell the difference between those who want to change and those who don't. I want to help people who want to be helped.

Talking to people about their stuff is fascinating to me. And while I advise clients to release judgment and emotion from things that cannot love them back, the process is easier said than done. People are often more attached to their things than they are to other people. The nostalgia of a dress from a first date or a project file from a career success often evokes more emotion than the person on the date or the coworker who shared in the project.

As I meet more and more clients, I am continually surprised by how much the average person needs to accomplish

to stay ahead. This busy society, with all of its technology and conveniences, has disabled many of us from achieving the basics of life, or what I like to call everyday maintenance. The idea of normal becomes relative. Living among piles of clutter is normal for a hoarder. Stashing thousands of dollars of misguided purchases is normal for a shopaholic. Working all hours of the evening and weekends is normal for a workaholic. For many, the clutter becomes the excuse for why they can't go for that job promotion, move out of their apartment, or end a bad relationship.

I have heard the who-has-the-time-to-get-organized excuse too many times to count. However, when time is dedicated to sort through their piles of memories, clients find more than an organized space; they often lay bare obstacles that have been holding them back. And the truth then becomes clear: *It was never really about the stuff.* In creating my company, **order.**, I have developed many consistent principles that help clients appreciate their lives more deeply. The true goal of all this stuff management is to find more time and space to focus on what is important to them. Without order, prioritizing is more difficult. Sure, I appreciate a genius filing system or a beautifully organized spice rack more than most. But my work is about what you gain, not what you purge.

Learning to let go of excess wants, along with the things, can actually result in more of what really counts — more living, more loving, more meaning.

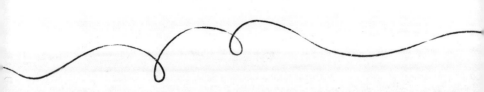

Ritual

THE OLD ADAGE that practice makes permanent is true. Anything that you give consistent attention to over time will become a cemented habit. Yogis know this; they have been practicing the same poses for over two thousand years. Whirling dervishes know this; they spin with a purpose, the speed of the spin bringing them closer to enlightenment. Christians, Muslims, and Jews know this; they regularly go to a church or mosque or synagogue to worship. But ritual is not always a religious practice. Olympic athletes have a routine of regimented practice and weight training. Opera singers practice scales and arias daily. All of these people share ritual; they practice to make their good habits permanent. And while most of us are not training for a gold medal in ski jump aerials, we each have our own goals to strive for, and those involve consistent effort over time.

The beginning of a new year is usually when people adopt new habits — or, in a more familiar term, make resolutions. They address all the new rituals they will put in place when the calendar page switches over and plan for the new routine to literally take root overnight. But like countless resolution makers before them who have failed and failed again, some annually, they quickly learn that changing a mindset and a way of life does not come with the end of one year and the beginning of the next as if a switch were thrown. Anyone who has started the cabbage soup diet on January 1, then crashed and burned on January 4 can attest to this. Good habits take time; while the beginning of the year is the start of a new daily planner, it does not always equate to the transformation of a new you. The date is arbitrary. In reality, every day presents the opportunity for a fresh start.

Recognizing that the underlying theme behind resolution making is flawed is the first step.

Vowing to make swift overnight changes is unrealistic and impossible to sustain. Like a child when his toys are taken away, you approach the weeks like an avaricious little rebel. Instead of setting up a feeling of deprivation that accompanies resolution making, choose to cement a ritual that you can live with, day in and day out. Removing the sense of deprivation will give you a much better chance at succeeding. This subtle shift in thinking is the key to maintaining good habits over time. New Year's resolutions do not work. The only annual resolution to make is resolving not to make them at all.

THE WAY
Lose the all-or-nothing mentality that resolutions engender; instead, practice daily rituals that slowly take root over time.

DAILY PRACTICES

✓ Let go of the idea of the calendar date marking when you begin your transformation. Instead, choose a slow and steady approach to achieving your goals. Rome wasn't built in a day, and you won't be ready for a marathon overnight, either. Remember that practice makes permanent.

✓ Recognize the Mardi Gras mentality that might cause you to yo-yo from one extreme to another. If you are an all or nothing–type person who is either bingeing or fasting, seek the middle ground this week by journaling what your imbalances are. Once you have recorded an oppor-

tunity for change, slowly adjust your habit to be worked on over time.

✓ To your own calendar be true. Do you have any rituals that you honor and practice daily, such as a walk at lunchtime or calling a parent every evening? Recognize your ability to make things that are important to you a priority, and begin to carve out the necessary time to honor them each day.

✓ Pause to value each day in the process of your new ritual. So much of our time is spent aspiring to the next level that we rarely celebrate the moment that we are in. Think of your process as charms on a bracelet, with each charm having its own intrinsic value. Being present for the daily moments will make you appreciate your efforts that much more.

✓ Be selective. Most of our promises to do better in the new year fall short because we simply choose too much to do all at once. Guarantee your success by being single minded: focus on becoming better at one area or task in your life. Do not give in to your knee-jerk reaction to list 10 resolutions to fix ASAP. Pick one or two areas to improve on over time.

✓ As you look at the good habits you want to foster, also review the bad habits you have cultivated. Letting something go at the start of a transformation is as powerful as taking on something new. Review the rituals that may have become harmful, and choose one to release.

2

Procrastinators, Read This First

IT'S 10 A.M. on a Monday morning, and I am cleaning my desk from top to bottom. On the surface this looks like a productive use of my time. But I am a writer on deadline. Now, I generally love deadlines; it is how I earn my living. The "assignment" as starting gun usually motivates me — but not today. Instead of organizing the thoughts in my mind, I am organizing the files on my desk. Telling myself that it is easier to work in an orderly environment, I put off my assignment, opting to do something more enjoyable — and more tangible — than the necessary project at hand.

Making a conscious choice to do something more pleasurable over a less-pleasurable task is the definition of procrastination. My inner procras-

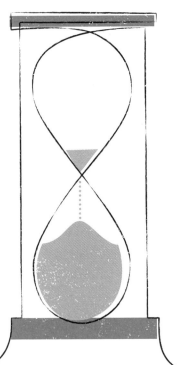

tinator has won temporarily, convincing my inner writer that a neater desk will make the process easier. For now, my inner writer waits outside the office as comfortable-avoidance mode sets in. When I procrastinate, I organize — unlike most people, who opt to surf the net, sort laundry, or phone a friend to put off life's sticky matters for a few more minutes or hours. Regardless of what you're procrastinating about or how you do so, the result is the same: avoiding what needs to be done. And while these little sidetracks cause instant gratification, they often create more trouble later.

Procrastination studies say that the relief is only a temporary fix. Ultimately, procrastinators feel even more pressured and frustrated for having delayed the inevitable. Procrastination also puts off productivity and accomplishment. Take my situation. With only two hours left to complete my assignment, my inner writer has reappeared and is growing increasingly uncomfortable. She is back — and she is not alone. My inner organizer has joined her, quickly remedying the situation with a stern reprimand and a door slam. Now fully present in both writing and organizing modes, I am relieved to be doing, not avoiding. My inner organizer urges me on, promising a tasty little reward. The sooner the assignment gets done, the sooner I can return to a more pleasurable task, like rearranging my e-mail files or rotating my winter sweaters. This reward is enough to keep me going through the morning!

> **Ultimately, procrastinators feel even more pressured and frustrated for having delayed the inevitable.**

THE WAY
Understand that procrastination is an avoidance behavior whereby a more pleasant task is selected over a less-pleasant task that brings relief in the short term but creates more mental anxiety and physical stress in the longer term.

DAILY PRACTICES

✓ Begin to identify your avoidance behaviors. Key phrases like "I work better under pressure" or "I am not in the mood today" put off the necessary aspects of life and create an unnecessary time crunch. Note when and why you do that. Being aware of how frequently you use avoidance behavior is the first step to changing the way you approach work and life.

✓ Ponder the classic story about meditation, wherein a student laments to a teacher that he has no time in his busy schedule to meditate. The teacher simply answers, "Meditate, meditate, and meditate." Follow this practice today by engaging in activity rather than passivity. Tell your inner procrastinator to wait outside till you have completed your work.

✓ Too much forward thinking — concentrating solely on how something will turn out — disengages us from the process necessary to complete a task. Cite examples of how forward thinking has caused procrastination. If you are waiting for perfect conditions to exist before beginning a process, you may never get started at all. Let go of the idea of success or failure, and revel in the act of *doing.*

✓ Be a thoughtful tortoise. If you recall the famous fairy tale, you know that slow and steady always wins the race. Take the race one lap at a time by breaking a project down into small tasks. Achieving interim goals will help you reach the finish line in your own time.

✓ Instead of delaying making a pesky phone call or attacking a junk-filled office, make that nasty task Job One today. Life is a reward-based system, so set up little goals and rewards along the way to aid in your progress. For example, once you cull your files, treat yourself to a fancy set of file folders. Having something to look forward to after each goal is met encourages steady progress. After all, we don't eat dessert first, right?

✓ Are you beginning to view your schedule and responsibilities differently? Examine the notion of your deadlines and other demands that are imposed on you. Set a comfortable pace on how you approach your work. Say a farewell to avoidance behaviors for good. In doing so, note the amount of time, space, and clarity that is created.

3

Do Not Delay Your Decisions with Clutter

A NEW CLIENT tells me that he is really good at organizing: He has every box, bin, and storage bag available. He has sorted, stored, and categorized every aspect of his life: his papers from high school are in one corner, his family photos are in another corner, and his tax files from the early '80s were recently moved under the kitchen table. He has no problem with clutter. He knows where everything is. As I am left wondering why Mr. Organized needs me, he explains the purpose of his call. Moving around all those neatly labeled boxes and bins has become difficult, and he wants help moving some of his tidy boxes to one of his storage units. Aha! The clutter plot thickens. He has more than one storage unit, a common trait of hoarders.

I go to his house and find a maze of Rubbermaid bins lining the walls of every room and hallway. He is indeed super organized, but he is super cluttered at the same time — a true organizer's dilemma. Everything is sorted and labeled to perfection, but he has fallen victim to the biggest culprit of organizing: he has created piles and piles of delayed decisions. He has simply relocated his clutter from room to room, from box to box, and eliminated nothing.

> Having the confidence to begin making decisions means choosing action versus inaction.

I can appreciate the hours of work it took to get this system arranged, but I am certain that most of what he has stored is unnecessary. I know this in the pit of my stomach. Like when your best friend asks advice about lending her boyfriend of two weeks a thousand dollars, you just know it is wrong.

Mr. Organized has only put his work on pause. He continues to ignore the years of decisions that should have been made: articles meant to be read, untried workout plans, letters needing answering . . . the list goes on. Consider all the decisions you make, from choosing a career to choosing a movie. Making decisions is part of life. We make them all the time. And they require focus, forethought, and assessment of personal goals. Having the confidence to begin making decisions means choosing

action versus inaction. Conversely, clutter is the antithesis of decision making. When we decide to do nothing, clutter piles up. Clutter management is a process free of editorializing. Clutter will go wherever we tell it to go.

Mr. Organized has actively stored his clutter, but he has not dealt with it. He did take the first and most necessary step: recognizing that something had to change. And although his solution to move boxes to another location is faulty, he *has* made an appropriate decision to look for a different way to manage his piles. And you can do the same. Eliminating a junk drawer, junk closet, or even a full storage unit with unknown contents is a good way to measure if you are eliminating clutter or simply storing it.

Often what holds us back is the guilt we feel about letting something go. But the items that we store and move from place to place are often of no use and arguably impossible to find. Employ the lens of "use it or lose it" to determine what needs to go first. Another common excuse is thinking that something will be needed in the future. Follow that line of reasoning by asking these hard questions and answering them truthfully:

- Will I ever use this item again?
- When was the last time I used this item?
- Does this item work?
- Is it outdated, broken, or ill fitting?

If you are honest, you will see that your clutter is not essential because you are not using any of it. We can usually determine its importance with one question: Have you ever missed something you let go and then been unable to replace it? Be candid. I have yet to have a client or student provide a concrete example of this. Consider the replacement factor here. Few things are irreplaceable, and more often than not that is what makes up our clutter. Instead of pushing clutter from home to home, room to room, or storage unit to storage unit, open up to truthful decision making. You will gain the power of not only being in control but also creating space, time, and energy in your life.

> **THE WAY**
> Practice active decision making, and become emboldened by the power you have over your stuff. Once you flip from passive to active mode, you will be able to live simply with less clutter.

DAILY PRACTICES

✓ ~~Albert Einstein~~ *Freud* noted that the definition of insanity is doing the same thing over and over again and expecting different results. Are you following a consistent clutter pattern in your life? Notice habits that are limiting you, making you feel anxious and distracted.

✓ Take a reality check of where you are with your clutter today. Have you moved it from place to place and avoided making a final decision? Take control over your possessions rather than vice versa. If you have a place where unknown items reside, take inventory, and eliminate the unnecessary.

✓ Consider what your motivation has been to build up this clutter, and realize that much of what delays your progress lies in excuse making. Starting now, make a conscious effort to eliminate the habit of excuse making. Put your items on notice, and recognize when you have kept something inactive for too long.

✓ Set a time limit on how long you keep certain unused things. If you have not used it within that time frame, let it go without exception.

✓ Clutter clearing evolves. Only you can find a solution that works for you over time, so use trial and error rather than following a cookie-cutter idea that may work for someone else. Believe in your power to change. *To conquer clutter, be aware of the journey, not the destination.* Consistent practice will return the most benefits.

✓ Envision organizing as a daily ritual like exercising, walking the dog, or brushing your teeth. This mind-set will help you find time every day to engage in clutter clearing.

4

Remove the Obstacles

AT 32, CYNDI became the vice president of one of the country's most prestigious public-relations firms. She made a lot of sacrifices to get there — going without vacations, family, kids, even a pet. She had little time for anything but climbing the corporate ladder. When she was let go rather unceremoniously as a result of company layoffs, no one was more shocked than Cyndi.

It was the first day back from the long Labor Day Weekend, and although her workday had started almost an hour earlier, she was summoned to the executive wing at 8 a.m. over what she assumed was the next pending public relations crisis. But a publicity crisis wasn't the problem; Cyndi was being fired. In minutes, her life had changed. She went from being the girl with the keys to the executive office to being escorted out of the building with her Rolodex and a picture of her with the president of the company. Her former assistant later sent Cyndi the contents of her fifteen-year career in several boxes, which now lined the hallway of her classic-four apartment.

After a bit of soul searching, she was ready to get back to work, and she decided it would have to be on her terms. She could not handle the powerlessness she had felt after her layoff. But Cyndi could not get started in her job search. In four months she had done little other than locate the packed Rolodex and place it atop those bulky office boxes — past reminders that she bumped into every time she walked in

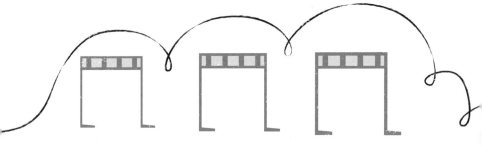

and out of her apartment. It was no wonder that she was unable to see her future. Obstacles can be challenging, but according to Ganesha, the ancient Hindu god of success — the elephantine deity frequently seen at the entrance of Indian restaurants — these obstacles are often placed to stop and make us think about where we are going. Cyndi was stuck and was not going to go anywhere until she dealt with those boxes that were literally and symbolically impeding her path. It was time for her and Ganesha to get together for a thoughtful review.

Over the next few weeks, although it was painful, she sorted through the boxes and the remnants of her corporate career, among them annual reports, pictures from the company picnic, and the yearly accolades for service. She began with 20 boxes, and by the time she had dealt with every piece of paper and every emotion associated with it, she was left with only two that held relevant content. Eighteen of those boxes were associated with her past, not her future, and they had to go. To celebrate, she invited a few close friends for a paper-shredding party; they said a proper good-bye to the old career and toasted a new era. Then Cyndi purchased a fancy new filing cabinet and several shiny white hanging folders in which to place the still-useful tools from her former work life. She was finally beginning to see her new path — and a clear hallway.

THE WAY

Leaving something behind can be difficult, especially when it is not your choice. Knowing that each step in our lives better prepares us for the next step can help turn a disappointment into a springboard for greater success.

DAILY PRACTICES

✓ Sometimes obstacles are placed in front of us to slow us down and make us take notice. Reflect on your life, and notice when a job loss or relationship ending has disappointed you. When things begin to leave your life, it is the universe's way of readying you for the next step. Learn how to let things go with grace.

✓ Be mindful of how sacrifice and deprivation work in your life. Depriving ourselves of things necessary to our well-being often causes a chain reaction down the road, requiring the playing field to be leveled. Be aware of feeling disappointed, and try to achieve a comfortable balance where you feel fulfilled, not lacking.

✓ At times our emotional side makes us hold on to things just for the sake of holding on. To make room for your future, you need to let go of things that serve only your past.

✓ Nostalgic thinking makes the past look better than it was — as if the future wouldn't ever compare. Be cognizant of your romanticizing past situations, and take comfort in knowing that you have the power to create a future on your own terms. Retire the Monday-morning quarterback for good, and readjust your practical side to move through situations with purpose.

✓ If you've lost your job, take stock of your skills and strengths. Use this time to decide if you want to reenter the workforce in the same profession or try a new career that may fulfill you more. Consider this time as a golden opportunity to home in on what you really want to do.

✓ Keep active and social. We often fantasize about the
day when we will have time to do things that work never
allowed us to do. Now you can. Take a class, reconnect
with friends, and recharge your batteries with a long
overdue vacation. Consider the notion of pampering
yourself as necessary preparation for life's next great
adventure.

SOME MIGHT CALL me a self-improvement junkie; I love taking workshops, believe in astrology and numerology, practice yoga, and often buy books on how to be a better businessperson. So when Oprah lauded the latest sensation, *The Secret*, as I was taking a teleclass on the law of attraction, I knew that there was no coincidence. After

The Law of Subtraction

all, I have read *The Celestine Prophecy* and believe as strongly
as James Redfield — and Sigmund Freud before him — that
in life there simply are no coincidences. Everything happens
for a reason.

This open approach has not only boosted my awareness
but also made me receptive to new philosophies. It is no
coincidence that attraction — the latest installment in self-
improvement — came to me as if I had, yes, attracted it. As I
penned in the dates for the weekly seminar into my datebook,
I noticed that it coincided twice with my bimonthly meditation class, and while I did not want to pass up the opportunity to attract the next best thing in my life, I also did not

want to jeopardize the progress my chi had made. Though my Zen master instructed that suffering was part of existence, I was not certain that this qualified. I was schedule conflicted and wondered if I had become a self-improvement magnet. To attract, I would have to do the opposite: subtract. Luckily, the first class was not a conflict; I was able to join my fellow classmates on an attraction conference call.

Our first assignment was to create a gratitude list. Mine was lengthy: my patient husband and energetic toddler and a career that allows to me spend time with both, our cozy urban apartment and its cool furnishings. . . . I was really rolling by the time I included the latest season of *Project Runway* and my shiny new MacBook computer. This exercise made me wonder if I had room in my life to attract anything else.

> The timing can be tricky, but abundance waits for no man.

Perhaps even this class was too much? The instructor taught my fellow callers and me that the world is abundant with opportunities. But we all signed up for more, more of everything. When you believe in abundance, you know there are no shortages. Like Jell-o, there is always room for more. This philosophy is especially effective when talking yourself out of buying another perfect little black dress that you convince yourself you will never find again. My attraction teachings reassure me that I can indeed

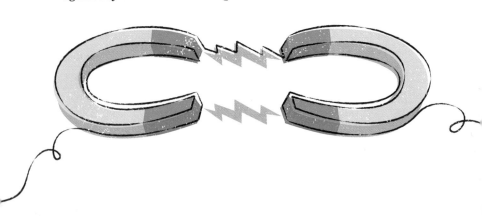

find another perfect little black dress and to walk out of the store with confidence.

With those lessons, gratitude inventory continued as a necessary life practice. And even though I was not leaving room to meditate, practice the downward dog, or read the latest Eckart Tolle book, I was confident that, like finding a little black dress, there would be no scarcity of time to accomplish all with a little tweaking here and there. I hit the refresh button on my day planner and juggled a few dates to make room. The timing can be tricky, but abundance waits for no man. So with a refreshed calendar and one fewer meditation class, I recycled my schedule, which made me feel eco savvy and evolved at the same time, as if I was actually using what I already had.

And for me that is the essence of the evolution: building on what you have, not adding for the sake of adding. It's like when you become an avid reader; you realize how much you haven't read instead of noting the books you *have* finished. So my self-improvement journey continues with an equal balance of all things abundant. Sometimes I add a new practice, and other times I take one away. I ebb and flow like the tide as needed. Because I believe that everything happens for a reason, this approach is probably no coincidence.

THE WAY
Self-improvement evolves, at times adding a new practice and at other times eliminating what no longer works. Keeping an open mind to knowledge in all of its forms will open you up to unforeseen growth opportunities.

DAILY PRACTICES

✓ Analyze your approach to life. Are you in "addition" mode with too many activities, books to read, and classes to attend? Pause and evaluate which ones hold the most meaning now, and embrace them with your full attention and energy. Once your evolutionary step is completed, you can move on to the next level.

✓ Allow a space for quiet gratitude in your everyday routine. Beginning in a place of thankfulness will help you gain appreciation for those blessings that are often taken for granted.

✓ Change your approach to the world by employing a glass-half-full mentality. When we dwell in the negativity, we are not able to see anything but obstacles and become part of a vicious cycle of negativity. Breaking this pattern will allow you to attract better experiences, relationships, and activities.

✓ If you tend to attract the same kinds of experiences, relationships, and situations, it might be time to recalibrate your energy. Follow the law of attraction, where like attracts like. Giving what you want back is the new golden rule.

✓ Be mindful of letting space enter your life and not filling it up too quickly. Dwell in the white space, and let something leave your life quietly before seeking a replacement. Acknowledge the gaps in your schedule, and thoughtfully fill them when the time is right.

✓ Practices that are important allow your individual spirituality to take root. Suddenly you realize the things you need the most. Let the knowledge of teachers guide your journey, but feel comfortable taking what you need when you need it. Not every school of thought is one you should be a student of.

EVERY CARD PLAYER has a "tell" — a twitch or a smile or some other subtle movement that lets you know that the player is bluffing and gives you all the information you need to win a hand. When "Filene" from Brooklyn calls, I am ready to listen to her specific project, but what I am really listening for is her "tell."

6

Possession Obsession

She explains she needed to call after finding my website online. Filene is a self-proclaimed shopaholic, which she shares with me proudly. *Most* good shoppers are proud of their skills, telling you about a designer bag snatched from the grasp of another Loehmann's customer or an Armani pantsuit scooped up for 40 percent off at the Barney's warehouse sale. These clever shoppers have refined a societal art, and Filene is clearly one of them. But within five minutes of our phone call, I realize that she never played poker; if she did, she did not play very well. "I read in an article that you are a recovering shopaholic," she says. "It is really hard for me to make this call, but talking makes me feel better already. I have already started taking your advice. I have been really good this week, and I haven't purchased anything new . . . this week."

And there it is, the tell — it's Tuesday. The tell does its job, helping me to determine that Filene is a shopaholic. Shopaholics are always looking for a deal, a coupon, or a discount. Why do you think DSW has a frequent-shopper card? Shopping is reward based, and Filene is looking for a similar pat on the back after spotting my recent online special. Her current restraint only leads me to believe that a couple of days prior, she was ensconced in the clearance rack at her local T.J. Maxx store. I am immediately suspicious of her sudden need to reform. This impulsive decision making could be what makes her a good shopper, but she could simply be looking for a new way to spend money.

"Can I buy anything new for your visit?" she asks. "Maybe a few hangers . . . shoe boxes . . . organizers . . . anything?" This conversation leads me to believe that decluttering is not her goal; Filene simply wants an excuse to buy more stuff. She is obsessed with possession — and in the process she has purchased me, a brand-new organizer.

THE WAY

Take a break from spending by buying only what you absolutely need and only when you absolutely need it. Differentiating between thoughtful purchasing and frivolous amassing is the barometer for measuring shopping's hold over you.

DAILY PRACTICES

✓ Evaluate your motivations for shopping. Outside influences like catalogs, Internet ads, and television can be strong motivators to purchasing. Switch the motivation to inner desire rather than outside stimuli, like a sale or promotion.

✓ Recognize your usage of the word "need" in your daily life. Often this powerful word is applied to nonessential "wants" and can be contagious. Use it correctly and sparingly. Wants are what turn good shoppers into shopaholics. Establish a true need or expressed purpose for every item before buying it.

✓ Peer pressure is pervasive in high school, but some battle it later in life, as well. Look at your peer group to determine if they are encouraging your purchasing habit. You can always shop with your friends, but you don't have to buy what they buy if you don't need the item.

✓ Turn to your daily planner, and note how many social activities revolve around shopping. If you were to eliminate those plans from your calendar, what activities would be left? Now note if some friends are just shopping buddies. In the process, begin to assess the activities and the time spent on accumulating rather than enjoying.

✓ Do you buy the same item over and over again without realizing that you already have these same items hanging in your closet? Begin to notice your repetitive purchasing patterns, and eliminate them. Temptation can be overwhelming when sales abound. Release the knee-jerk reaction to stockpile.

✓ Practice conscientious returning: make sure that the things you buy, you wear. Subscribe to the rule of buying with a purpose, and if you do not wear the item within a reasonable time span, return it. A good gauge is within a week or two.

7

Contain Yourself

CLIENTS OFTEN ASK me: What do I need to do before your visit? Should I straighten up? Run to the Container Store? Buy more space bags? The overwhelming desire to reorganize always comes with the hidden agenda of purchasing new things. When you think about it, how do you really know what containers you'll need if you don't know what you'll be containing? The Container Store is my favorite place on earth; it is nirvana for the organizer, but it *is* a retailer, designed to sell and make money. And how they make money is to create a need for the prettiest shoe storage boxes to house your fifty or one hundred pairs of shoes.

But the question we need to be asking is not in what do I store my fifty pairs of shoes but why do I have fifty pairs of shoes to begin with? Do you need fifty or one hundred pairs of anything, really? Sure, we can contain anything; there is a box, bin, or file cabinet to house everything — from the sublime (a CD binder that allows you to ditch those dreadful CD towers and all those pesky plastic jewel cases) to the ridiculous (a gift-wrap work station; who gives that many gifts?). And this is the case for most organizing; we see an opportunity to upgrade our stuff by buying a different kind of stuff: *organizing* stuff. We fall into the same cycle, putting our consumerism into action — which is how we ended up with all this clutter in the first place.

For example, for a local magazine piece on a home makeover, I put out a call to my community website clients

regarding interest, and the e-mails and phone calls flooded in. And virtually everyone asked, "Will you buy all the stuff we need to make over the room?" Most people think, "Make my stuff look prettier" when they should be thinking, "I need to pare down, not rearrange it better." We all have too much stuff. This is a well-studied topic. One survey found that, on average, people only use about 10 percent of their wardrobes — and I suspect for women it might be even less. And how many rent storage units to store offseason clothing? So let's readjust our thinking when it comes to organizing by first containing yourself and *then* containing your stuff. Only when you have paired down to the essentials should you head to the store. Your slimmed-down pile of stuff will dictate its own needs.

THE WAY
In our consumerist society, the inclination is to purchase to make things better when more purchasing actually creates disorganization. Instead of increasing your storage, decrease your stuff.

DAILY PRACTICES

✓ Shift your thinking to one of necessity by keeping only what you use. Thoughtfully study the most disorganized spaces in your house or apartment, and determine if reorganizing is really the solution or if less stuff is what is called for.

✓ Don't be romanced by the availability of pretty organizing products. There are as many crafty solutions as there are inventors that make them. For every thing in the house, someone has thought of a way to store it and store it better. Making something's packaging more appealing is not going to make you suddenly use the item more often.

✓ Some items are obsolete — for example, the plastic-bag storage system. Ultimately we should be using reusable bags for all purchases, which can be reused in every area of life. Kick plastic bags to the curb, and save the environment while you are at it!

✓ Gain familiarity with your things. A lot of organizing schools of thought emphasize flipping hangers when an item is worn and other clever tricks to help us remember what we really use. Can you begin the process of knowing what you have by putting your items together in categories and determining what you need to live on a daily basis? If you have too many unrecognizable items, storing is not your solution, purging is.

✓ Hone your editing skills daily. If you keep putting on the same ill-fitting sweater hoping that somehow the shape will now flatter you, let it go. Items like this are not worth keeping, much less storing.

✓ Beware the storage facility! If you are pushing things out of your house thinking that you will eventually use them, you might be hooked on a costly practice. True, some occasional-use items like camping equipment or holiday decorations should be stored. But when your storage unit becomes too big, it is time to reevaluate the necessity of those items.

8

The Not-So-Instant Makeover

A JENNY CRAIG commercial advertises "Lose 20 Pounds for $20." This advertising message convinces us that the instant fix is possible. We watch ambush makeovers, total house renovations, and millionaire matchmaking, which change people's lives in one episode. Our time-pressed society has a time limit for these renovations to reach completion. A British nanny, a confrontational chef, or a genius life coach makes your house, your body, or your life perfect. However, real life is nothing like so-called reality television. If it were, overnight we all could look like Heidi Klum, design like Jonathan Adler, and cook like Bobby Flay.

Still, TV makes all this seem possible. We intuitively know this but still resolve on January 1 to eat nothing but celery and train for a marathon, even though the brownies you just made are not going to disappear on their own. Every time we think of change, we plan for the extreme make-over. For example, my brother Joe, whom I call "Yo-Yo," is diligent about going to the gym, watching his calories, and attending Weight Watchers meetings. When he falls off the wagon, he then yo-yos and goes on an insane three-day diet that is so detailed in its timing, it is nearly impossible to follow. On this diet he eats metabolically balanced foods — such as vanilla yogurt, two ounces of meat, peanut butter, and small pieces of fruit — at specific intervals throughout the day.

> Real transformation does not take place overnight or in an hour or instantly; it must be cultivated and worked on daily.

I have witnessed this cycle countless times, which renders Yo-Yo hostile and not suitable for social interaction. And although it is not pleasant, he muscles through it. But the reality is that the extreme discipline of the three-day diet cannot be maintained over time. The euphoric thinness gives way to overconfidence and lax habits, and he soon reverts to the other extreme. Before you know it, he is taking third and fourth helpings of our mother's eggplant and is back where he started. Yo-Yo needs a lot of food; were he not so interested in his appearance, he could easily become a competitive eater. When he is not dieting, I usually have to guard my plate against his stealth fork, which silently pounces on my

mashed potatoes. I used to enjoy going to dinner with him for the favorable results on my own figure. He eats faster than I do and usually will guilt me into sharing.

Pendulum dieting is not a healthy approach to weight loss but one that exemplifies how many people approach change: If I can just dedicate three days — or three hours or three minutes — everything will change. Life is not the quick fix it is on television, where experts sweep in to guarantee results as well as ratings. And while watching reality TV gives us a sense that we are not alone in our personal challenges, these shows are primarily entertainment. Many of these experiments should not be tried at home because real-life results vary. When you plan your makeover, keep it real by making subtle shifts that cement permanent change. Altering ingrained habits is hard work. Real transformation does not take place overnight or in an hour or instantly; it must be cultivated and worked on daily. Although that may not make for great television, it can certainly change your life.

THE WAY
Life-changing makeovers take time and commitment. Removing the word "instant" from our expectations will help us reach and maintain our goals over time.

DAILY PRACTICES

✓ Banish instant gratification from your vocabulary. You did not become overweight, overcluttered, or overstressed overnight, so understand that a solution will take equally long to instill. Readjust your goals to manageable ones that you can chip away over time.

✓ Understand that self-improvement is a process, like a chain of events where actions and experiences build and build till the ultimate goal is achieved. Make a plan with smaller sustainable steps that will take you out of the instant-makeover mind frame.

✓ Don't try to fast forward to the end result. Often we are focused on the "reveal" moment that glosses over the actual work it takes to lose that 15 pounds or to wade through accumulated high school memorabilia. Real work is an essential component to change and can sometimes be challenging and uncomfortable.

✓ Setting realistic goals at the beginning is the first step to any transformation. Crafty television editing does not show the setbacks that occur on the way to growth. Doing your best the majority of the time will cement good habits that will help you overcome setbacks.

✓ Attitude is everything. Looking at lesson four, have you become someone who will easily give up? This week, practice getting back on the treadmill when minor setbacks derail your journey. Life is full of detours, but getting back on track consistently reinforces success.

✓ Surround yourself with supportive people. If you have a friend who encourages you to eat Big Macs and shop the sales, you might want to take your pal to yoga instead. Begin to analyze the things in your day that contribute to your bad habits.

Attachment

FOR ANYONE WHO has ever cared for a child or even babysat a child, they know the challenge of getting little babies to sleep. And as a new parent apparently looking like I was in need, I was constantly on the receiving end of unsolicited help and advice. Well-intended friends and family sent books, e-mailed articles, and shared sage advice about naps, schedules, and crying. But the one piece of advice that I found the most fascinating, given my career choice, was a friend who asked if my son had a "wooby."

Anthony clued me in that a wooby is "the thing they cannot live without; the only thing that gets them to sleep." Now, my four-month-old baby had no attachments at all at that point — although I had to admit that creating a connection to a wooby at three in the morning did seem like a good solution for the entire family. I was also told to give the baby a pacifier, which I tried, but my son shot that thing across the room like a rocket and never looked back. So a wooby seemed like a bit of a stretch. But more than the notion of finding something for Matthew to get attached to, I questioned the notion of

creating the attachment to begin with. Is this where all of our stuff worship originates — with a wooby?

I couldn't help but imagine what cave people did about woobies. And this reflection is one I always come back to: What did our foremothers do without these modern tools seemingly necessary for child rearing? It is amazing that any of us lived, based on the lack of safety inventions available back then. Yet we survived and thrived, maybe through pure instinct. Babies are resilient. I wondered if I'd had a wooby that would perhaps explain my attachment to things in my adulthood — namely Gucci shoes. Perhaps my baby booties were my attachment item, my wooby.

Attachment is a learned behavior, and as is the case with any less-desirable habit that has become detrimental, it is one that can be unlearned, as well. As adults, we are constantly learning and unlearning new skills and habits. Applying this to our present personal-attachment items, we can begin to address what we can live without and, in turn, shed. We begin to wonder if we ever needed our adult woobies to begin with.

Does losing a particular possession cause you to have a sleepless night? If so, you should examine your attachment to your stuff. Yogis practice detachment from physical possessions to achieve clarity. I suggest that we all should apply this ancient wisdom to the way we relate to our things.

THE WAY
Attachment is a learned behavior that you can unteach yourself and easily modify with practice.

DAILY PRACTICES

✓ Identify the things in your life that you can live without by separating the emotions you attach to those things. Journaling your observations will help shed the light.

✓ Challenge yourself this week to release a thing's grasp over you. Is that third cup of coffee spiking your energy in the afternoon, or are you taking part just to keep a coworker company? Just because we have always done something does not mean we have to keep doing it.

✓ Nature versus nurture is an important lesson in early-childhood development. Observe this in your adult life by recognizing how the people around you influence your lifestyle, whether it's your best friend, an office mate, or even a parent. Some habits have become second nature, picked up from those around us.

✓ I take a tip from the yogis by practicing detachment and, to identify your abilities to do without, by looking within.

✓ The idea of attachment can often lead to addiction, so be mindful of the warning signs when there is something in your life you absolutely cannot live without. A crutch can be easily developed, tipping the balance, so realize when more becomes too much.

✓ Context is important. Think about the many world lessons perceived from such disasters as Hurricane Katrina. Life-altering events offer a sobering reality check on what's important. If you are connecting too much with the material world, remind yourself of what is truly valuable and what is ultimately replaceable.

10

Real Life Happens from A to Z

I LOVE *REAL SIMPLE* magazine. Its beautiful photographs of ultraorganized rooms provide inspiration for its many devout readers. Despite the succinct title, the magazine is chock full of hundreds of suggestions, ideas, and solutions every month. *Real Simple* and other decorating magazines are inspirational, offering the reader a dizzying amount of suggestions that range from A to Z. To sort out the right project for you, think of organizing as a continuum like the alphabet, with *A* being the least fastidious person and *Z* being . . . well, the editor of *Real Simple.*

Understanding where you stand within this alphabetic spectrum will help you pick and choose what projects to attack and when. And only you can determine which endeavor works for you. Compare this to how you approach your diet, your exercise program, or your work philosophy, all of which call for personalization. Organizing is the same; it begins with assessing your personal goals, followed by committing the time to complete the project. Magazines are wonderful places to find ideas and know-how, but keep in mind that they are meant to appeal to a variety of people at various stages in their lives. Having a discerning eye when reading these glossies will allow you to let your inner needs guide your path.

A good example is the scrapbooking craze. Many are intrigued by the idea of capturing life's wonderful moments with copious documentation — ticket stubs, photos, train tickets, playbills, and the like — and some may be tempted to create a book for every year, every vacation, and every family member. Maintaining a hobby like scrapbooking is clearly a *Z* activity, requiring the most detail, the most upkeep, and the most time. Constant maintenance is often required, making it easy to fall behind. So if the kind of detail that scrapbooking requires is not your style, find something easier to maintain like a digital album or even a photo storage box. A project should be easy to keep up and bring you pleasure, not anxiety. Once the work becomes arduous, we are less likely to continue, regardless of what we think the ultimate payoff will be. In the end, half-started projects clutter our closets. Before beginning a new project, evaluate the time commitment, the maintenance requirement, and your desire to complete the project.

Before beginning a new project, evaluate the time commitment, the maintenance requirement, and your desire to complete the project.

My client Ellen is known as a serial starter; she often finds inspiration to begin a project but rarely finishes. At a recent session we spent a few hours carving out space for abandoned hobbies, including sewing, knitting, quilting, and jewelry making, none of which had been touched in several years and I was doubtful would ever be touched again. Yet she was influenced to start more and more pastimes. I explained to Ellen that she can admire a hobby without having to participate. Instead, pause and reflect before heading out to the craft store, and make a plan to ensure a project's success.

Asking a few questions before beginning enables you to choose the right activities and bring them to completion. Satisfaction of a project done well is the goal rather than disappointment for failing at a too-lofty enterprise. Ellen and others like her learn that customization is the key to success. Personal style and habits are the barometers for your hobbies, not pressure to conform to another person's way of doing things. When you read home-improvement publications, keep a careful eye out for things that are intuitive to how you work and live, and apply them to your life. You can always wait for next month's issue for inspiration that's a good fit. It is just that simple.

THE WAY
Ignore outside portrayals of how other people live, and embrace your style and habits in a realistic manner. Comparing your lifestyle to others' creates a false illusion. Instead, let your inner needs and work style guide your project selection.

DAILY PRACTICES

✓ Consider your elements of style by knowing what works for you, what habits you practice daily, and what motivates you to create order. Good habits breed more good habits. Assign a letter of the alphabet to where you are today.

✓ Let go of the notion of the perfect way to live, and begin to embrace what is perfect for you. Organizing, like life, is not a one-size-fits-all proposition, so think customization rather than conformity.

✓ Consider your motivation for starting, then stopping new projects, and evaluate why some projects did not keep your interest and were abandoned. Determine whether you are influenced by outside stimuli rather than inner passion.

✓ Notice the amount of "some day" projects you have lined up that will occur once you get organized. Are you planning for the future rather than living in the present? If you are setting up unrealistic goals for yourself, realign your thinking to more practical steps.

✓ Look to home design magazines as ideals to guide you to the next level, not intimidate you. Life always looks better when professionally photographed, so use these photos as inspiration, not pressure.

✓ Has your pie-in-the-sky thinking been given a real simple reality check? Make a solid plan for completing your projects by evaluating your time commitment. Use past project success and failures as a guide. Be inspired to become a project finisher, not a serial starter.

11

Upside Downsize

EVERY SO OFTEN a new word becomes part of the lexicon seemingly overnight. Many words adopted by corporate America have become common out of the boardroom, too. Some good examples are "partnering," where two business professionals get together to achieve a common goal, or "multitasking," which once referred only to a computer's ability to perform many tasks simultaneously and now refers to anyone's ability to juggle a number of tasks at one time.

Perhaps the pièce de résistance is "working lunch," which allows workers to combine both partnering and multitasking while ingesting a meal.

Such double-duty language leads me to believe that we all have too much on our collective plates. This is certainly true of a word that is now so yesterday. "Supersizing," a logical progression for those working lunchers, quickly came into fashion, causing many to order up simply because they could. I ask those "supersizers" to consider the next big word — or at least the next small word — in need of an extreme makeover: "downsizing." The time seems right to downsize our supersized portions and cappuccinos, a move that will help not only our waistlines but also our wallets. When my company downsized me rather abruptly, it put an end to my corporate life for the foreseeable future.

A friend once told me that all things end when they should, which left little excuse for me not to pursue more rewarding career ambitions that were shelved while I was living in the supersized corporate world. But there were a couple of holdouts from my Fortune 500 self: two pantsuits that lurked in my closet. Justifications for keeping the suits were multiple: they were expensive, they were Armani, and they could be worn again. Even though I had not worn them in four years, I could not let them go. Help came from a fashionista friend, who made me model the two suits for her. The reflection in her mirror revealed the person from my past, not my future. And with that realization, I released the two suits from my present. I found them a good home at a local woman's shelter; hopefully, one of the temporary residents would land a job wearing my Armanis.

Passing these suits on to someone just starting her corporate life provided the closure I needed. I left the shelter with a sense of relief; the downsizing of wardrobe now matched my life. When unused items go somewhere happy, you don't feel so bad. Pass it on.

THE WAY
Plan a closet-review session, complete with a fashion show. Have your friends be judge and jury. Only keep the items that look the best and suit your life *now*. Let the rest go. Chances are they will be perfect for someone else.

DAILY PRACTICES
✓ Make sure you are seizing the moment of today, and ask a trusted and stylish friend to review your collection. Be certain that your wardrobe fits your here-and-now lifestyle, not one befitting who you once were or who you think you should be.

✓ Consider the ease in your morning routine. If finding something to wear takes too much time, slowing you from getting out the door, organize. The real estate mantra of "location, location, and location" applied to your closet will help you get dressed effortlessly. The most-used pieces should be the most accessible.

✓ Identify the top-10 "cannot live without" pieces and the bottom 10 that are of little use. We only use a fraction of our clothing, so identify little-worn items, and create closet karma by passing them on to a local charity that can put them to good use.

✓ Reframe the way you shop by purchasing pieces that are the most flattering, that fit you now, and that are age appropriate. Create a signature style rather than keeping up with the latest runway trends.

✓ Each time you wear a favorite piece, revel in the notion of reuse, and celebrate this good purchase. Having tried-and-true garments that make you feel great is a reward in and of itself — plus it's easy on your pocketbook. Keep this in mind when you shop in the future to avoid buyer's remorse.

✓ Stay engaged with your possessions by consistent purging, editing, and maintaining. Keeping everything in working order will create more options for dressing. Always shop your closet first before heading out to purchase a one-time-wear outfit.

GARAGE SALES ARE a great way to divest no-longer-wanted stuff. In cities where there are no garages, resourceful urbanites sell their unneeded coffeemakers, Tolstoy novels, and vinyl records on the sidewalks in front of their apartment buildings to passersby — so-called gate, or stoop, sales. Plentiful foot traffic

12
Previously Owned

can result in a very successful sale. Plus it's fun to meet your neighbors and enjoy a final cup of tea outside on your old beach chair — until you sell it, of course.

My friend Ted loves garage sales. He is always looking for unique, interesting finds. He found a rare amber Tiffany lamp, which he paid a Pier 1 price for. But more than the actual piece, Ted likes the interesting stories that accompany old things.

Ted relocated from New York City to Canada to open a new office for his company. Knowing that he was there for a short period of time, he acquired little. He got up to speed quickly on Canadian roads with the help of several atlases. (This was in the days preceding the however-did-I live-without-that GPS.) Two years later Ted was moving back to New York City and freed himself of his Canadian gear, selling what he couldn't use and donating the rest to a local charity. On the way home from a farewell lunch with his boss, he passed a stoop sale. Fully aware that he should be in shed, not accumulation, mode, he nonetheless could not resist the temptation to browse. Ted reviewed the collection of books and CDs displayed on a red-and white-checkered tablecloth (which was also for sale) and was drawn immediately to the road atlases, recalling his first days in Canada when such guides were his bible.

While basking in nostalgia, he noticed something familiar about these particular maps as he flipped through them. The copious Post-it notes that were attached to the dog-eared pages seemed to correspond with routes that he had driven himself. What are the chances, he thought, that someone may have traveled the exact same routes? He looked further at a city map, which also had familiar dog-eared pages and highlighted markings. More clues emerged. His subway stop was labeled. His house was highlighted. These were *his* maps, the ones he had deemed unusable and threw out the night before when packing the last of his things! Someone wanted them — specifically, wanted to sell them — markings and all. When he relayed the story to me, it all seemed so eco, so urban, and so industrious. It is true that one person's treasure can be another person's trash, but it is also true that in this new world of commerce and exchange, sooner or later we just might end up with our same old stuff. Ted passed up on the opportunity to buy his old maps again. But he never passes up the opportunity to tell this good story.

THE WAY
Conscientious resale and recycling can often lead to a disposable mentality. Be thoughtful when determining if something has run its course; then prepare to set it free.

DAILY PRACTICES
√ Garage, yard, and gate sales are terrific ways to make money on unused and unwanted items as well as to get necessities at a discount. Take advantage of garage sales to find what you need at a value price.

✓ Green is good; recycling and reuse have become vogue. Many household items can get a new life when looked at differently. A steamer trunk as a filing cabinet? Baskets for storage and waste? Consider repurposing and refreshing your objects before letting them go.

✓ Live by the adage that one person's junk is another person's treasure. Finding new homes for your no-longer-needed items has never been easier, with websites like Craigslist and Freecycle. And the best part is that people will come to your house and pick them up.

✓ Practice thoughtful consumerism by buying what you need when you need it. Garage sales are great ways to pick up bargain items, but the high of the bargain is addicting. Be choosy; otherwise, you may need a garage sale of your own.

✓ Purging is essential to good housekeeping. Incorporate shedding the unused, worn, or torn into your housecleaning routine. Using an editing eye when cleaning your house not only creates space but also makes upkeep much easier.

✓ Enjoy the pride that comes with not being wasteful. Shift your focus to use, not purchase, making sure you are not buying multiples of products that already reside in your cabinets. Change your inner mantra to "I used all of that," rather than running to the store to purchase a replacement before you truly need it.

13

Get Comfortable in Your Own Clothes

SHOPPING THE MALLS of New Jersey in my teens set the foundation for my fashion-obsessed adulthood. My fascination for clothing often put me not only into my own closet, where my not-so-secret shopping addiction was best evidenced, but also the closets of friends and family, where I began to learn more about them than just their shoe size or affinity for pencil skirts. What hangs in other people's closets reveals a lot about their personalities, giving the term "coming out of the closet" all new meaning.

My own self-discovery began in my closet and worked its way out to every other aspect of my life — a makeover that led to a career change, a marriage, and the purchase of a home. Closet makeovers are why I started order in the first place. After spending most if not all of my free time shopping for bargains and then finding pretty ways to store them, I know the joys of clothing maintenance.

Alicia is a stylish 42-year-old woman who always looks great and whose sense of fashion I have always admired. So when the opportunity arose to help her sort out her closets, I jumped at the opportunity. When Alicia called for help, she was looking for more than new hangers. Alicia's posh Westchester home has many closets, including a master walk-in closet with a center island and a large wall of shelving to house her hundreds of pairs of shoes. (This closet is larger than many city apartments.) In the downstairs bedrooms, she housed her off-season clothing and her formal wear. A third cedar closet in the upstairs office stored her coats.

"Let's start with your master closet, the place you get dressed everyday," I suggested. "These items are everyday items, and they should be accessible. Pick the place that annoys you the most," I offered. This technique of "show me where it hurts" is often the best starting point for jobs of this size. Alicia's choice was skirts. "Take them all out," I told her. We unloaded 35 skirts onto her king-sized bed — 35! I ponder this number; how can one woman need 35 skirts? I ask her to pick out the ones she wears. She selects 4. When I ask her what the other 31 are doing there, she explains that skirts varied in size from 4 to 14. She kept this range of sizes as her weight may fluctuate. Keeping fat clothes and thin clothes is a common habit. (Alicia is presently a healthy size 10.) The real dilemma has emerged.

"When was the last time you wore a size four?" I asked. She admitted that it was the fall of 1999, when she was persuaded by her sister to do the Atkins diet. "Why are you no longer on the Atkins diet?" I questioned. She tells me that she had liver dysfunction as a result of too much protein. After she passed out in a department-store dressing room, her doctor added more carbohydrates to her plate. She loaded her diet with pasta and bread, and by the following year, she was wearing a size 14 and was through with extreme dieting. Now she takes a more balanced approach to eating and exercises frequently. As a result, for three years she has maintained her shapely size 10, a natural weight for her height and age. The only purpose left for those size 4 skirts was to taunt Alicia on a daily basis, reminding her of the person she once was. And honestly, being starved on a bacon-only diet is not a great memory, anyway. I tell her so.

Size keeping is a habit prevalent among women who are desperate to recapture their smallest size — as if having the

size 4 in your closet means that you are actually wearing it. Alicia's natural size is a 10, yet she was housing a wardrobe she can never wear. Slowly, we released the extreme sizes and made way for what fits her now. Her closet was still full of fashionable choices, and Alicia was relieved to see those size 4s and 14s out and the healthy middle range grown. Setting up false ideals that can never be met is a common pitfall when selecting a wardrobe. We often think that we will someday fit back into something, but all we are doing is causing frustration and unrealistic expectations. Freeing herself from thinking that these clothes would be worn again enabled Alicia to appreciate who she is today. Just as her diet was brought into balance, so was her closet. And she realized that size really does not matter.

THE WAY
Romancing the idea of a slimmer, younger you prevents you from embracing who you are now. Inhabit your body and mind by respecting the steps that brought you here.

DAILY PRACTICES
✓ Bodies change over time. What you once wore in high school is not going to fit you as an adult, plain and simple. Recognize that a certain amount of weight gain comes with aging, see it as a necessary part of the process, and keep your expectations realistic as you age gracefully.

✓ Note the pieces in your wardrobe that bring guilt, shame, and nostalgia — sometimes even regret. Address the

emotion behind the keeping, and let go of the item with its accompanying emotion. If letting the unused items go brings sadness, keep a memory of those fashions by snapping a photo and donating the piece to someone who can use it.

✓ Maintaining your closet goes hand in hand with maintaining your weight. Use the mantra of healthy living, not extreme dieting, when thinking about your clothing, and be consistent with your diet routine. Nothing looks better on a healthy body than simple pieces that fit.

✓ Rotating seasonal clothing in and out of your main closet is the best way to keep closets orderly. You will create more space by keeping only the current season in your closet and storing winter sweaters at the top of the closet or in clever under-bed storage. Keeping everything in one closet can make decision making confusing and time consuming.

✓ Try a few tried-and-true storage solutions if you are challenged for space. Use luggage for off-season storage; it's a great way to use something you are storing anyway. A double hang bar instantly doubles your space.

✓ Arrange your closet by keeping the most-used items handy. Items like formal wear, fur coats, and costume pieces have no place in your everyday closet, so find them a new home in a spare closet or storage box.

Honor Thy Memory

AUNT BESSIE WAS everybody's favorite. She always told wonderful stories about her travels abroad and her time as a USO performer during World War II. But the thing that everyone will remember about Aunt Bessie is her literal head-to-toe fashion, topping every outfit with a coordinating hat. By the time she passed away at age 87, she had amassed quite a chapeau collection, and everyone wondered where her hats would go. She and her great-niece Chelsea had a special bond; they often went out for tea, giving Aunt Bessie the perfect opportunity to showcase her many different hats. Chelsea loved to see which hat Aunt Bessie would wear: peacock feathers, pink sequins, or even black sable. Chelsea remembered them all.

Not surprisingly, Aunt Bessie willed Chelsea the collection. And while Chelsea had no idea what she would do with 75 hats, she felt as if discarding them would be equal to discarding Aunt Bessie. Though she had no room in her small home for the hats and their coordinating boxes, Chelsea thought that giving them away would not honor the close relationship the two had shared. Perhaps she could fit in 10 or 5 or 2. . . .

But do those hats really replace Aunt Bessie, and would giving them away dishonor Chelsea's memory of her relative? I pose this question to my workshop students, and by a show of hands I make the following suggestions: Who would keep them all? (One or two people sheepishly raise their hands.) Who would keep a few? (More people raise their hands.) Who would keep none? (Not one hand is raised. In

the future, I may need to make the Aunt Bessie story a bit less emotional.) And then the big question: Do these hats really represent Aunt Bessie? (Some holdouts say yes, but most have turned the corner to separate the loved one from their loved *things*.) I ask a few follow-up questions. Can you preserve the memory of a loved one by not keeping every memento? Can the memory be cherished by a few things as well as many?

Can you preserve the memory of a loved one by not keeping every memento? Can the memory be cherished by a few things as well as many?

We get to work on finding a thoughtful memorial for Aunt Bessie and her chapeaus and come up with some great suggestions: Donate the hats to a local theater group; sell them to an antiques shop and donate the money to a charity in Aunt Bessie's name; and the best, contact the teahouse where the twosome enjoyed so many afternoons about displaying the hats as an ongoing tribute to their loyal customer. These are just a few ideas that truly honor the memory of Aunt Bessie. In the end, we all agree that to keep a memory alive, you need to honor the person above her things.

> **THE WAY**
> Losing a loved one can be hard. Our instinct is to keep everything they owned out of respect. Realize that things can represent people but do not replace the emotions, experiences, and love you shared.

DAILY PRACTICES

✓ Take the following keepsake quiz: Do you have treasured items in a storage bin, attic, basement, or even a dresser drawer? Are you sharing these memories with friends and family? Asking questions will help you determine how to locate, treasure, and honor your family's keepsakes.

✓ To help find out more about your treasures, take the importance test. If you had to leave your house unexpectedly and could take only a few items with you, what would you take? Most of us can answer this question easily: a wedding album, a high-school yearbook, jewelry, a stamp collection. Now set a time limit for locating these items. While this extreme scenario is one we hope we will never encounter, it is a good test of how accessible our prized possessions are.

✓ Letting go is often difficult, especially when we've inherited possessions. If your house has become a shrine to those who have passed, it is time to lighten your load. Balance your respect for a person by keeping a small sampling of their belongings, not every memento.

✓ Get creative with a true memorial that creates a legacy for the person, like an ongoing charity or annual family get-together for tea. Memory keeping comes from lively stories so that the person's accomplishments and experiences move forward, not the possessions they accrued along the way.

✓ Photographs are the most-kept mementos. Make organizing these a priority by choosing acid-free boxes or photo albums, and get sorting. (You can even scan an electronic version of a favorite photo to use for note cards or holiday greetings.) Thoughtful frames and shadow boxes put photographic memories front and center.

✓ Spread the wealth. It seems that one family member often becomes the recipient of all the housewares and mementos as if there can be only one family historian. Instead, spread the wealth among your relatives. Passing mementos on to loved ones makes memory keeping a group activity.

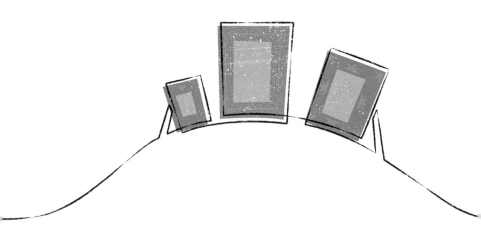

15

Something Is Missing

ORGANIZED PEOPLE ARE often met with skepticism — as if we are so tidy we can't be trusted. Whenever I tell chaos junkies what it is I really do, I am always up for the inevitable challenge. These people will tell me that their genius filing system of putting all their papers on the floor is just the way they like it. They claim to know where everything is. They even claim to be more creative. I know there is more here than meets the eye, and it is now my job not only to defend this new industry making its way into society but also to inform them of the underlying bonus to organizing. It is not about having the cleanest desk in the office or owning the coolest file folders that you can find at Target (although both make me euphoric). The goal is to find more time to do the things you want to do.

Clients usually come to me when they have a nagging feeling that something is missing. They may be living a life that is unfulfilled — or to put it in the words of the first organizer, Henry David Thoreau, they are not "living the life they imagined." (Comparing myself to Thoreau also makes me euphoric.) Like HDT and me, these clutter bugs want to live the life they imagined, but their clutter is taking too much time to manage and sapping them of the energy they need to do anything else. The end result: clutter wins out. And when you have a clear-cut winner, there is usually an equally clear loser. My goal is to find that loser and give it a voice.

The entire organizing industry is founded on the notion of saving time and money, not that we should be neater.

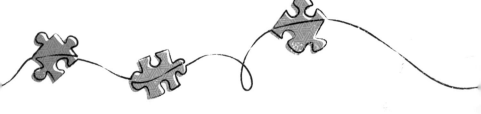

(Though in the process, everything looks better.) By saving time and money, you attain the goal of doing something of your choosing. When we rid ourselves of clutter stress, we open ourselves up to all new possibilities. People who crave order and clarity are usually feeling an imbalance in other places in their lives. Self-improvement TV shows give us insight into the imbalance. We watch the single girl who wants desperately to get married but refuses to go on a date, the miserable corporate worker who thinks he has to settle for an unsatisfactory career, or the picky house hunter who wants a mansion for a bargain.

> Clearing the clutter is a means to an end and perhaps the first step in any real transformation.

It is obvious to the viewer that they all share a nagging feeling that something better awaits them. What motivates change in all of these people is the desire to find that missing piece, that something they don't currently have. And that is the benefit to getting organized; it helps us see our lives for what they really are, without the distraction of clothes, papers, or collectibles. Clearing the clutter is a means to an end and perhaps the first step in any real transformation. Change often begins with an inner voice that silently whispers. But organizing helps that voice speak volumes.

THE WAY
Knowing that change is on its way is signaled by a desire to want more of the right things and less of the things that don't make you happy.

DAILY PRACTICES

✓ Are you stuck in a rut: the same unsatisfying job, the same unsatisfying relationship, or the same unsatisfying place to live? Are you settling for a less of a life than the one you imagine for yourself? Take a clean sheet of paper, describe the life you want, and compare it to the life you are currently living.

✓ Review the exercise you did yesterday. Can you find the missing elements of your life? Do they cause you discomfort? Or were they once part of your life and are now lost? Make a list of the things you want to be doing instead of the things that are overshadowing. It is time to focus on the elements of your life that are losing out.

✓ Now that you have identified the things that matter most to you, make a contract with yourself to start today on a new goal: to make yourself happy.

✓ Clutter clearing affords us the opportunity to see clearly without distraction; it helps us gain focus and perspective. But sometimes it is helpful to talk to someone who can offer advice. Consult a local organizer, life coach, or trusted friend to talk through what is holding you back.

✓ Rid yourself of the negativity and complaints about your current situation by changing your viewpoint. A positive outlook powers change.

✓ Understand the link between language and attitude. Rather than using words that are self-defeating, phrase things positively, which reinforces your power.

FROM FACEBOOK TO *Real Housewives,* everyone seems to be complaining about something — but what is really at the core of this unrest? If we believe the law of attraction, we realize that all this unhappy talk will only lead to more unhappiness. But breaking a habit that feeds itself is hard. It might take deconstructing relationships that fuel our desire to vent.

16

To Complain Is Human; to Stop, Divine

A good example comes from Renee and Rosy, two employees who were laid off from the same company on the same day. This experience created a very close bond based on a common enemy: the past employer. They needed to mutually voice their frustrations, form solidarity, and make themselves feel better about their sudden dismissal. They spent most of the winter months verbally tearing apart their former office and the coworkers who did not get laid off, then found that they could complain about the process of finding a new job. Although neither wanted to return to their former employer even if they could, the grass proved no greener at the countless interviews they went on. They frequently met to recount their latest disappointments, their conversations revolving around complaining about the things they could no longer do.

This cycle continued for a full year, and in a way it was good that the women had each other to see themselves through the inevitable dark period. But sooner or later you have to, as they say, take out your own trash and move forward with your life. Renee, an administrative assistant, was ready to move on first. She hired a career coach to sort through not only her job goals but also her life goals. The coach helped her to identify all the positive attributes she possessed and find different fields where those skills could be applied. As a result, Renee focused on getting an advanced degree in veterinary medicine, a big career change that would not happen overnight. Simultaneously, a former colleague offered her a position at a new firm, so she would be able to pay her way to her new vocation.

> Always remember that misery loves company, and if you choose not to be its friend, perhaps it will go away.

When Renee told Rosy about her exciting career change, she was taken aback by the reaction. Rosy complained about the person who was hiring Renee and told her negative things about the new company she was to work for. Things were not quite as rosy for Rosy. She had done little to forward her job search since the layoff and instead focused on getting together with former colleagues to gossip and complain. Her cycle had not yet run its course — but her friendship with Renee had. Without the common bond of misery, they had little to say to one another. In fact, Rosy told Renee that she felt betrayed and hurt that Renee would not spend as much time with her talking about the old days. Sadly, Rosy was emotionally stuck, and her old life continued.

When Renee made a positive change in her life, the complaining ended and good things began to happen, proving that complaining and negativity feed more complaining and negativity. You can be a Renee or a Rosy. Always remember that misery loves company, and if you choose not to be its friend, perhaps it will go away.

THE WAY
While some complaining is inescapable, constant complaining derails your ability to be happy.

DAILY PRACTICES

✓ The common misconception that venting will make you feel better is not true. It feeds more of the same. Note the difference between productive explanation and useless complaining — and eliminate the latter.

✓ Examine the relationships in your life that foster complaining. We all have a work colleague whom we vent to about the boss or a family member to vent to about our spouse, best friend, or even a sibling. Are these relationships solely built on complaining, and if you were to eliminate the "vent" session, would anything be left? Replace pessimistic conversations with constructive problem solving, not negative gossip that gets you nowhere.

✓ Complaining often comes from being self-absorbed rather than self-aware. This week, practice emotion-free judgment when analyzing a situation, and take the high road. By eliminating our ego from the situation, we get closer to achieving a good solution.

✓ Analyze your media intake; many outlets exist to give you a false sense of importance by pointing out others' flaws. Be wary of the tabloid-journalism effect in your own life, where scrutiny and criticism direct the way. Lead with a compliment or kind word instead of a slam.

✓ When a bad situation happens, move out of "why me?" mode by deciding not to be a victim of your actions. While a certain amount of wallowing or grieving is neces- sary, it is only one stage in your development. Honor the emotion, but if it begins to impede your progress, release your inner victim with the help of your inner warrior.

✓ Focus on your assets by taking stock of the things you do well, that you love, and that you want to pursue in the future. Realigning ourselves after a letdown can be done with the constant practice of positive thinking. Let your assets unlock the opportunities that await you.

WHEN THE RECENT economic collapse created one of the worst recessions since the Great Depression, many people panicked, losing all faith in their government, their employer, and their bank. My circle of friends was not immune to this panic; some stockpiled cash

Downshift

in their apartments, fearing that the ATMs would suddenly stop dispensing cash.

This was quite a change from a short while earlier, when record home sales and unprecedented economic growth was taken for granted. Some of us chose to ride the wave, upgrade our technology, live above our means, and charge more than we could afford, buying into the pay-it-later mentality that fuels our economic system. Everything was affordable, making the possibilities endless. Buying a house for half a million dollars at 4.5 percent interest rate, even if you had no down payment, made perfect sense at the time. The banks trusted that you could pay the monthly mortgage. Now we are still hung over from that spending party, stuck with a huge tab and forced to live a less-excessive lifestyle. The concept of "less is more" is new to many, but it has been taking root in some circles for decades.

In February 2006 I was asked to write a front-page commentary on the topic. Though the world had not yet undergone its economic seismic shift, mine had already changed. Up until that point I was a corporate city girl, adding outfits and martinis to an already complicated lifestyle. As a shopaholic in recovery, I was challenged by the editor to write about the future of less. The piece detailed the six areas where less was better: less big business, less technology, less

accumulation, less clutter, less distraction, and less weight. I systematically took each area and assessed how much was too much. I described how I had downshifted from the "addition generation," whereby adding more and more to my already full life was not resulting in anything but an increase in distraction, confusion, and credit card bills.

My conscious decision was to sacrifice — which isn't necessarily a negative. Initially some might feel deprived of their creature comforts, but that is soon replaced by an increased sense of meaning, appreciation, and clarity. I eventually devoted my work to the pursuit of less and helping others to create more meaningful relationships in their lives — essentially to get on with living and learning instead of spending and amassing. The article closed with a prediction about the future of less, quoting philosopher Lao Tzu, who said that in order to shrink, we first must expand.

And that is exactly what is happening now. We have expanded every aspect of our lives, and it is time to shrink back to the essentials. Casting a wide net often helps us to focus on what is important. As for the future of less, I see it this way: Less shopping and credit-card use leads to less clutter, less accumulation, and less debt. Less gluttony leads to less hunger. Less waste leads to a cleaner planet. Less stress leads to more meaning. Fewer cars lead to less pollution. Less terrorism leads to more peace. The world looks pretty good with just a little bit less.

THE WAY
Too much of anything clouds our minds, our homes, and eventually our planet. Let finding the balance between what you want and what you need guide you to living an informed life with less stuff and more meaning.

DAILY PRACTICES

✓ Understanding the difference between needs and wants is essential when taking inventory in your life. When you measure your possessions, your activities, and your life choices by this barometer, you will see what you can live without.

✓ Your credit card bill is the best way to find out not only where your money is being spent but also where your time is being spent. Look at your monthly bills, and notice if something is out of balance. If you're buying things that you cannot actually afford to sustain a particular facet of your life, perhaps that facet is an overpowering money drain. Find your hidden money pit, and adjust your spending accordingly.

✓ Examine the role outside influences play on your spending. Does advertising become the decision maker for your choice of car, bedroom carpet, and restaurant? Understanding how external influences abound in this society is the first step to making decisions that reflect your need, not someone else's want.

✓ Deprivation is a feeling of helplessness, where we are thrust into a situation not of our choosing. Sacrifice, on the other hand, is in our control, a powerful choice that leads to growth and enlightenment. Take control of your life's choices, and leave feelings of deprivation behind.

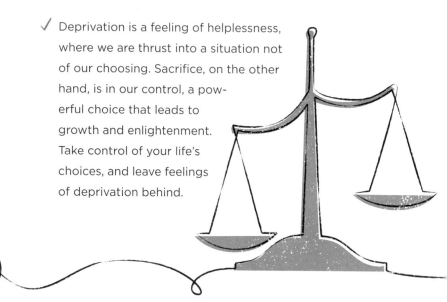

✓ Take a spending break in all areas of your life; forego dining out, gourmet coffee, and designer shoes. This seemingly extreme practice will help you get a handle on where your money is being spent and point out what is necessary and what is unnecessary.

✓ Appreciate and be grateful for what you have. A philosopher once noted that if we were to throw our problems into a pile with other people's problems, we would gladly take ours back. Put on the rose-colored glasses this week, and become the architect of a future that builds on what you have learned from your past.

18
Love Things That Love You Back

IN A PRETTY apartment on the pretty Upper East Side of Manhattan, a not-so pretty battle was taking place. The scene: a large walk-in closet strewn with handbags, shoes, and clothing. The characters: a shopaholic and an organizer. The conflict: finding room for all the merchandise. "I *love* this bag," explained the shopaholic of her Coach purse. "I could not possibly give it up." Score one for the shopper. Next article, a briefcase, also Coach. Again, deep proclamations of love. "This briefcase is Corinthian leather, and I *love* Corinthian leather!"

As the organizer coaxed the shopper to get rid of something, *anything*, a theme was starting to emerge. This shopper was in love with her stuff. This idea of loving things is very common — but can we truly love our stuff? Let's pause to define the term.

According to Webster's, "Love is a strong affection for another, arising out of a kinship or personal ties." By definition, then, possessions cannot be loved because possessions do not love you back. Try substituting "cherish" or "treasure" when praising your belongings because inherent in love is reciprocity. With that in mind, it is unrealistic to conduct so many one-sided love affairs.

But this argument is not really about semantics; it is about where we place our emotions. When using the word "love" to describe her objects, the shopper put up a roadblock that the organizer had to deconstruct. It would seem unfair, inhumane, or just plain cruel to separate someone from something they loved. But does she really love the item? Or is a lovely memory associated with the item that created the lasting bond — a first date with your now-spouse, a trip to Bermuda with a good friend, or a fantastic job interview? If the latter is the case, the emotion should be placed where it belongs: with the person or experience that brought the joy. Now let's go one step further. When was the last time you used the *L* word when thinking about that spouse, that vacation mate, or that boss who you made you so happy? When you look at your loving relationships through this lens, everything changes. Letting go of the intangibles allows you to focus your strong emotions on relationships, not things. If you truly love something, set it free — chances are you can find it again at the mall.

> **THE WAY**
> People who live in experience, travel, taste, and touch are natural explorers; they recount memories of things they have done, friends they have made, and places they have seen. Consider these memory gems your best-prized possessions; they go much further than any seemingly perfect purchase.

DAILY PRACTICES

✓ Notice your use of the word "love" in your daily life; assigning it to inanimate objects and using it too often may be lessening the effects of this very powerful word. Recognize the use of the L word by you and those around you.

✓ Take a field trip to your favorite store, and engage in the act of appreciation instead of purchase. Simply look around at the beauty of the clothing, the jewelry, or even the digital cameras. Think about your local shop as a retail museum where beauty is admired, not possessed.

✓ Review your weekly activities, and note if you have time to share, explore, and experience or if most activities are linked primarily to ownership.

✓ Review your monthly activities and expenses — how much time and money is spent cultivating love or being shared with a loved one. Seek out ways to remedy the imbalances.

✓ Begin to use the word "love" more appropriately, and find examples in your life of how your new view of love has changed. Next, identify an activity you love and thrive in the experience of doing and being.

✓ Now that you have recognized the love in your life and honor experience over possession, seek ways to pass it on. Activate the reciprocity of the emotion. A simple gesture such as a thank-you note or an expressed "I love you" to your best friend is contagious. Becoming a part of the love chain reinforces the powerful effect of not only giving but also receiving love in your life.

19

"Order Is the Shape upon Which Beauty Depends"

I LOVE THIS quote by novelist Pearl S. Buck, not only because order is the name of my company and my personal mantra but also because it tells us that order is where everything begins. And this is true of any artistic venture, whether you are staring at a blank canvas, a blank computer screen, or an unfurnished study. The white space is important; it is the catalyst to creativity. Take interior design shows, where houses are cluttered beyond recognition, and then a savvy design team comes in to revamp the space. The first thing that they do is clear out the room to look at the space in its raw form. They know that chaos causes distraction and confusion, whereas an empty room permits the designer to see the multiple possibilities and explore every option clearly.

When too many things crowd our space, we become unable to focus, making beginning a challenge. And this is what Pearl S. Buck meant by looking at life as a raw space where once we clean the slate, we can then decorate, paint, write, or sculpt.

Nowhere have I ever seen this concept put into place more clearly than when I visited the home of painter Richard Pasquarelli, who was being featured in a home-design magazine I write for. His meticulously organized space had small shelves for paints and brushes, medium shelves for sketchpads and design books, and large shelves for canvas and frames. In the middle of all that order stood a large island, free of clutter, just waiting for Richard's artistic inspiration. The studio, which opened onto a garden, was flooded with sunlight. Even though my knowledge of the visual arts is very limited, I was awe-struck by the open flow of the studio and how it showcased his work. The focal point was a stunning painting displayed to its best benefit on a blank wall, able to be enjoyed and appreciated with no distraction. Richard is not only a great artist but also a foundation builder, designing the perfect space to seed his creativity.

His space impressed me so much that when I left I had a surge of confidence and actually thought I might try painting myself! And that is what a good artist, singer, or dancer does: they inspire you and give you the confidence to follow their lead. Richard is a truly inspirational artist. Any time I am ready to create or get inspired, I recall the foundation building that his art studio required, from scratch with the raw ingredients. All of us have the innate ability to start fresh with a clean slate — a tabula rasa. In more tangible terms, think of an Etch A Sketch.

THE WAY
When you begin with a raw space, you have infinite choices and possibilities to create your version of artistic beauty. Open space inspires us to build a world of our own choosing, so wipe the slate clean, and revel in your latest masterpiece.

DAILY PRACTICES

✓ Creativity is an essential part of our lives, whether we use our artistic side to build a tree house, sculpt a vase, or write a poem. Nourish your childlike ability to play in the white space. This week, take time for artful play without placing limitations or expectations on where the journey takes you.

✓ Identify a space in your home or office where you can start fresh. Commit to clearing the clutter and distraction, and make a space for your creativity to take root.

✓ Try this exercise: Sit in a familiar room and notice all the detail — you might even make a list of what is around you. Did you notice a photo of childhood friends or a piece of pottery that you have not paid attention to? Does that item look new again? Consider fresh ways of featuring items to better appreciate them.

✓ If your tendency is to crowd a space with too much art, take a cue from the artist's studio, and display one picture, one piece of art or even a swatch of beautiful fabric on white space. Note the beauty of a stand-alone piece. Create more visual interest by rotating your favorite pieces to keep the focal point new and interesting.

✓ In numerology, the number seven is known as the magician, a person who is able to create foundations wherever he is sent. He is not the type to worry about losing things, confident that he always has the power to rebuild. Harness the creative magician in you by being confident in your ability to change and evolve. Committing to something new will enable your inner magician to place beauty in your orderly world.

✓ Treat your life like an Etch A Sketch by constantly shaking up the chaos to create order. Starting over with a blank slate offers us chances to observe the beauty all around us.

IT'S GAME SEVEN of the World Series, and the Yankees are three outs away from winning the title. As I sit in the stands watching the final batters approach the plate, I am distracted. A fan sitting behind the plate is talking on his cell phone.

20

Be Here Now

My mind leaps to several scenarios that would make this kind of rude behavior acceptable: He is a doctor on a call with a colleague doing open-heart surgery, his wife is in a taxi and went into sudden labor, or he has just inherited a French chateau from his beloved Aunt Sophie and is arranging moving details. I could understand the need for conversation in light of these situations — at least the first two. Moving into Aunt Sophie's chateau could certainly wait a few more innings.

I am ruminating on how to justify his behavior when the final batter gets to the plate and takes his first strike. If we both don't focus back to the action at hand, we might well miss the play of the game, perhaps even the last play of the season. But I suddenly feel like I'm watching one of those reality television shows, like the latest installment of *Real Housewives.* The absurdity of those shows gives me higher ground, and I have that same feeling of righteousness as the caller continues to talk. I wonder why he cannot be in the moment of the game, in the now.

Likely, none of my above scenarios are true, and his call is simply frivolous. He's making plans for after the game or telling a coworker that he scored the company seats. *Hang up before you miss the moment!* I yell at him telepathically. Life is not like a DVR that you can rewind if you miss out on the action — a bad habit I have adopted when trying to catch

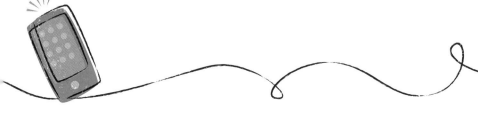

all the catty repartee on *Top Chef*. Perhaps the caller thinks that he can press pause and catch up on the action. And I have fallen victim to the same thinking since I'm watching the man rather than the action at the plate. But the truth is we only have one shot at this moment, and he is probably reporting it rather than living it while I am transfixed on what he will do next.

This "reporting" behavior is part and parcel to the age of the cell phone, where shouts of "Can you hear me now?" reign over every situation. We also seem to be unable to be on time because we know we can call and say we will be late. I think of all the calls I have made to tell someone I am three blocks away. Or the ones seeking advice on which iPhone to buy while at the Apple store — having placed the call on my current iPhone, naturally. These conversations are of questionable necessity, but they are infectious. We call, text, and blog, creating electronic chatter simply because the technology exists. But the technology may exist before a true purpose.

I focus back to living in real time — just in time to see Mariano Rivera throw the game-winning pitch, a high pop up to right field. Then I see the catch. The season ends. Did the caller see the play, or was he still on the phone? And since I allowed myself to be distracted by his cell phone usage, I am no different from him. Neither of us focused on the action at hand. Thankfully for me, I recovered in time.

THE WAY
Living in the moment — or as yogi Ram Das says, "being here now" — makes us more mindful of the beauty of everyday experience. Slowing down the pace of life to live from moment to moment creates an atmosphere where you can recognize and appreciate the blessings in your life.

DAILY PRACTICES

✓ Start the day with quiet reflection. Take a tip from the yogis, and set an intention to live in the moment. Now begin to eliminate any distracting thoughts. Take five minutes at the start of the day to think of nothing, ridding your mind of distractions.

✓ For many, a spa retreat is an ideal getaway that includes relaxing, quiet reflection, and escape from daily routines. Create a space in your home for a daily retreat: a favorite reading chair, a scented candle to invoke a sense memory, or even a photo of your favorite beach. Establishing a daily habit like a walk in the middle of the day or an aromatherapy bath at day's end can instill the positive effects of the spa into your lifestyle.

✓ Conducting multiple conversations at one time causes distraction, confusion, and eventually stress. Note the idea of picture in picture in your life, like a modern TV, as you juggle two competing tasks at one time. This task jumping causes the shortchanging of one task for another. Reflect on what this does not only to your productivity but also to your mental state.

✓ Observe your use of technology by noting the temptations around you. Become conscious of the impulse to tell someone about what you are doing rather than simply doing it. Note the subtle changes in your mood as you begin to become more present in your daily life.

✓ Practice focus and concentration by choosing one task to do for fifteen minutes. Set a timer if that helps. Notice the benefits of what you can accomplish with your new singular focus.

✓ People don't evolve as fast as technology. Consider your needs before upgrading for the sake of upgrading. Just because a camera has a 40X zoom lens does not mean you need it or should own it.

21

Invest in Experience, Not Things

I AM SEARCHING for the perfect gift for my best friend, Muriel, who is turning fifty. We have been friends for over 20 years and given and received countless cardigans, charm bracelets, handbags, and stationery. Each Christmas and birthday I rack my brain to come up with a unique gift. And each year it gets harder and harder.

Muriel and I have a lot of memories together, most of which recall traveling to our favorite destinations: the Napa Valley, Italy, and the Caribbean. Many times our travels were for birthdays. Staying home on these landmark days seemed insufficient — or as Muriel so aptly puts it, "Who wants to turn fifty in Connecticut in the dead of winter?" We didn't know it when we first started traveling as a way of celebrating, but we were on to a new trend: giving the gift of experience. Traditional gifts usually end up being used for a while at best and eventually get put away. Instead, we made memories that will last a lifetime. One trip we took together immediately leaps to mind. Muriel and I went on a harrowing hike in a Caribbean rain forest to a remote site to see petroglyphs dating back thousands of years that had been etched on the rock wall of a riverbank. The majestic beauty of the destination was worth the effort of the hike, and it was certainly an experience that we will always remember.

Soon after that excursion, while I was browsing in a local gift shop, I saw a ring depicting one of the ancient etchings, and the shopper in me emerged: I had to have it. When I returned home and wore the ring to my office, I received different responses about my shopping conquest. Apparently I was not the only one enamored by this ancient symbol. A colleague asked me, "Why are you wearing a ring with the Caneel Bay resort symbol?" I explained that it depicted an ancient petroglyph, one that I had, in fact, seen on my vacation, I boasted with a superior world-traveler-like knowledge.

A few days later, another work colleague asked about the symbol on my shiny sterling silver ring, and I happily

recounted the daunting hike and our arrival at the riverbank. This time the comment was not quite what I expected. "So at this riverbank, they had a gift shop?" she challenged. And I suddenly questioned whether I had simply found a new thing to buy to represent the experience instead of just living in the experience as it had been.

This push and pull is common not only on vacation but whenever we give in to a need to purchase a token of the event rather than simply enjoy the memory as it is happening. Our tendency is to commemorate just about everything we do. This is best evidenced by souvenir collecting, which capitalizes on our innate tendency to collect in order to commemorate. And while this is a nice hobby, it can result in cluttered homes. We begin to tie emotion to everything we do, whether that takes the form of a snow globe, a coffee mug, a kitchen magnet, or, yes, a piece of jewelry. We often need a physical thing to trigger the memory of our good experience. Whenever I sift through clients' boxes of such one-of-a kind mementos, I am struck by the money wasted on novelties.

Our tendency is to commemorate just about everything we do.

With that in mind, I begin to shop for Muriel. Research begins with the Internet, where I search for "living in experiences." Several websites suggest life-changing experiences from cruises to the Galapagos to in-home spa treatments and everything in between. Sadly, Muriel

and I are not in a place this year to take off on one of our famous trips, but I *can* give her something that would help her experience the sense of a getaway. I think Muriel, I think Napa — and the pop-up screen reinforces my thought bubble: wine, at home, concierge. Perfect! At-home tasting of Napa Valley's best! Coupled with this story, it might just be an experience of a lifetime.

> **THE WAY**
> When we focus on experiencing life, we create memories that have long-lasting meaning — unlike a purchase that may provide merely a temporary high.

DAILY PRACTICES

✓ Identify those times in your life that are rooted in experience rather than objects. Begin to think about your possessions in this context, noting if your emotional buying may be delaying your innate ability to experience the memorable moments. Make a concerted effort to amass experiences, not collectibles.

✓ Identify your gift-giving personality: are you someone who showers your friends and family with gifts or someone who shares in experiences to celebrate? Commit to a new approach. Planning a birthday dinner with friends in place of another scarf will give you all something to look forward to.

✓ The statement "the gift of your friendship" is not used often enough. Don't wait for a special occasion to employ this phrase; thanking a friend for being a positive influence in your life is something you can do at any time.

✓ Rewarding ourselves with gifts is common when we reach certain milestones — a new apartment, a new weight goal, even the conclusion of a hectic week. Consider replacing some purchases with experiences: call several friends, spend a few hours at the beach. When we emphasize "thing collecting," not only do we cheat ourselves out of sharing an experience with another, but also rewarding ourselves too frequently can lead to devaluing our possessions.

✓ Make your wishes known. Instead of feeling guilty about receiving gifts you will never use, let your friends and family know that you would prefer either no gifts or that the money be sent to a charity. This also eliminates unnecessary spending and clutter along with your guilt.

✓ Get over the guilt behind holding on to gifts that you do not want or will not use. Negative emotional keeping can clutter your house with things you do not love. While it is a delicate dance not to offend the sender, the only way to stop the inflow is to be honest about the item. You need not display every Precious Moments figurine that your cousin sent you.

THERE IS THAT famous Jack Benny comedy bit where a robber demands of Jack, "Your money or your life." Silence. The robber threatens again, "Your money or your life." Finally Jack responds, "I'm thinking it over!"

Opting Out

Making choices can be difficult, especially when they involve deep-seated behaviors. I am reminded of this when a new client calls for help with his clutter problem.

"How did you find me?" I ask Stewart. He says that his wife saw an article I wrote in the newspaper about clutter. "When she handed your number to me, she said, 'This is the only piece of paper I want you to keep. But you have to act on it.'" His demeanor is polite, with no humor or lilt to his voice. I have the impression that he is a professional person but that he rarely deals with clients or colleagues. I suspect this because he does not laugh easily; he is all business. Since this was not his idea, I am leery of Stewart's dedication to change. My experience has taught me that change usually needs to be an original idea, not one forced on you by a loved one, regardless of how well intended.

"I have a problem with paper," he explains. "Many do," I answer. I lighten the mood by assuring him that he has come to the right place. "I deal with paper more than I deal with any other clutter issue," I explain. "Paper love is common," I joke.

No response. He is going to be hard to break.

"What kind of paper are you referring to, personal or office?" His response: "Yes." This short answer leads me to believe there is much more than just paper here. "I have been struggling for a while now to get things organized." *Struggle* is another clue, the operative word when talking about making change. *Struggle* implies that the problem is so great that it renders you helpless. How can paper cause a human struggle? Man vs. god or man vs. evil, maybe, but man vs. paper? Other words can be used in this context, such as "control," "manage," or even "purge." He chose "struggle" — and then he drops the bomb by asking when I can come over for a cleaning session. "Cleaning" denotes a broad sweep into the garbage, something that paper lovers rarely agree to. I am intrigued but skeptical. Why now? After living in the paper jungle for so long, why is he finally motivated to change? Is the motivation his wife's alone? Or does he sincerely want to change his life? I play along, hoping that he loves his life — and his wife — more than he loves his paper.

THE WAY

Holding on to paper is a common tendency that creates a habit of proving ourselves: proof of payment, proof of where we have been, or proof of what somebody said. Turn this passive thinking around by finding the confidence in the person you truly are, not the person you are on paper.

DAILY PRACTICES

✓ Start classifying your paper into categories, such as nostalgic, financial, or medical. Organize the piles side by side to figure out if there are imbalances in one or more categories or if you are keeping multiple copies of outdated material.

✓ Consider the last time someone asked you about a bill payment. In the electronic age, payment can be proved via the Internet, a cancelled check, or a quick call to the bank. Rid yourself of mindless recordkeeping by being confident that you can always recreate a paper trail.

✓ Opt out online. E-mail inboxes have become the new place for clutter. You don't need every newsletter and retail announcement via e-mail, so decide what you will read. Be selective about whom you give your e-mail address to, and unsubscribe to nonessentials.

✓ Be leery of serial recycling. Consider the environment when you subscribe to magazines, and take the pressure off yourself to read your periodicals every week or month. If you are not reading your subscriptions, take a break from the commitment, and buy only the occasional single copy to read that you will enjoy. Placing unrealistic time expectations creates recycling piles, not reading piles.

✓ Turn your reading shelf into a home library by reading, then passing on books that you have read. Practice a rotation of "one book in, one book out." Make a new rule of not buying a new book until you complete the last one on your reading pile.

✓ Instill a good office habit in your home by keeping files. Choose a system that works for you and that you can maintain, whether it's a traditional filing cabinet, matching storage boxes, or a portable accordion file. Designate an area for personal papers, and store important documents like leases and licenses in a fireproof box.

23

Extraordinary Time

I WAS ALWAYS confused at church when the religious calendar would change back to ordinary time, which meant there was no special season coming like Easter or Christmas. Life would go back to being ordinary. The word itself means "of no special quality or interest, plain or undistinguished."

Talk about no fun. For me, this transition from special to ordinary was emotional. As a child, I cried when the holiday season ended — the tree would come down, the presents were put away, and all those Christmas cookies were gone. The anticipation of the extraordinary time had ended and with it no more expectation of great things to happen. We would go back to ordinary time, where day in and day out, things would be pretty ordinary.

But most of our days are of this variety, not special occasions like Christmas. As I got older, "ordinary time" became the day-to-day task management that we all do without fanfare or even recognition. Picking up the dry cleaning, dropping the kids off at soccer practice, roasting the chicken, cleaning up after dinner as the day quickly turns to night. We move through baby feedings, school report cards, performance reviews at work, birthdays, and college admissions . . . events all flow into one another. And with this flow, we take the ordinary for granted.

Perhaps inhabiting these ordinary days is the point. Our parents and grandparents, bolstered by the confidence of lessons learned though long experience, urge us to savor every day because the little baby who needs those nightly feedings will be leaving for college soon, and we will wonder where

the time went. None of this seems plausible; even though we hear it over and over, it still does not sink in. Perhaps perspective and understanding the true meaning of life are gained only at fleeting moments when a hard lesson is taught: the loss of a young life, the tragedy of a fire or hurricane, a loved one who suddenly takes seriously ill. All of these defining yet devastating moments give us an appreciation for the ordinary.

But why does it take that? I am reminded of my answer whenever people ask me how my flight was, and I am

We often jeopardize the joy of the ordinary moments because we are worrying about the future or belaboring decisions we made in the past.

always happy to report, "Uneventful." The report of the ordinary flight is the best report you can give. Our tendency is to jump ahead — when we work, we think about vacation; when we are on vacation, we think about the flight home; when we go to sleep, we think about the next day. It's as if our personal remote control is always fast-forwarding to give us a sneak peek at how the story will end. Finding ourselves so caught up with what has passed or with what is before us, we neglect the moment we are in; we lose that presence that makes us appreciate the first snowstorm of the season or the first time your baby smiles or your first real job or your first apartment — the list of gifts goes on and on.

If you take the advice of those who have more experience, they always say the same thing: enjoy it; it goes faster

than you think. We often jeopardize the joy of the ordinary moments because we are worrying about the future or belaboring decisions we made in the past. But the more that we can detach from these emotions, the more we can enjoy the present. Many psychologists refer to this as living in the flow of life. Taking this collective wisdom, how can we do anything but enjoy exactly where we are now, with the knowledge that it will all speed by *so* fast.

THE WAY
Mindfulness, or living in the moment, provides profound health benefits and promotes overall happiness. Become an observer of your thoughts, not a victim of them.

DAILY PRACTICES

✓ Each day this week, recognize at least one good thing that happened. Reflect on the ordinary moments in each day — something as simple as using a coupon at the supermarket or a stranger smiling at you as you pass on the street. Note the beauty of ordinary days, and note by week's end how you approach the flow of your life. You might just enjoy exactly where you are, wherever you are.

✓ Mindfulness, by definition, is detaching yourself from overthinking about the moment at hand. Are you living in the moment and letting life's flow embody you, or are you spending time thinking about how you feel about the past or future? Make yourself a third-party observer instead of the main protagonist.

✓ Are you the type of person who limits his or her behavior because of how you think you will look? Chances are no one scrutinizes you as much as you scrutinize yourself, so take the front position in aerobics class, and enjoy the freedom of being imperfect, as you exist now. People respond to truth and confidence more than anything else.

✓ Measure your anxiety level when a major situation arises. Anxiety increases when you overly think a situation. We trick ourselves into believing that the more we think through a situation, the better the outcome will be. Shift your thought process to *managing* the task at hand rather than how you *feel* about the task at hand. This week separate the two; the reward will be that the task never lives up to the torment you put yourself through.

✓ When you deal with adversity head on, you ready yourself for the next difficult situation that life hands you. You become prepared and confident rather than unsteady and fearful. Avoiding a conflict will only magnify an issue later on, so deal with that molehill before it becomes a mountain.

✓ Appreciation is the final step in this journey and one that we often recognize too late in life. Become an old soul this week, and make it a point to follow the sage advice of older family members. Plan a visit to reconnect either in person or by phone, and revel in their knowledge and experience.

24

Asset Management

YOLANDA IS A single woman in her late fifties who enjoys shopping, cooking, and traveling. (A recent trip was to Taos to paint landscapes.) She takes poetry-writing and knitting classes and loves to shop flea markets for bargains. Her home is filled with her finds — as well as bags filled with whatever incidentals she might have picked up on the way home. I work with Yolanda monthly, usually following one of her girl weekends.

While I'm sorting out her acquisitions, a startling pattern emerges. Yolanda tosses the change from a purchase into the shopping bag that holds the goods. A bag that contains gum, toothpaste, and Tylenol might also have three or four dollars in it. Every bag has to be checked for money. Most of the bags are strewn on the dining room table, where change mingles with mail and spills onto the dining room chairs and the floor.

Yolanda, who makes a nice living, has no respect for money. This is surprising for someone who is ultra put together with the latest styles — not to mention more than one beautiful leather wallet to house her hard-earned cash. Claiming her busy lifestyle doesn't allow her to put things back when she is done with them, she uses the plastic store bag like a tiny time capsule to hold the entire purchase instead of taking the time to return the money to her wallet.

My wallet habits were born from many hours of childhood Monopoly games with my financially savvy brother Matthew. He treated anything having to do with money and numbers with the utmost respect and would methodically count and

sort his twenties and tens. Like a teenaged Donald Trump, he built his hotels all over Atlantic Avenue and beyond. Today he is well in charge of his family finances and carefully invests when he sees fit. His money clip, like my wallet, is orderly, with denominations arranged in descending order. We respect our money.

When the experience is enjoyable, you are likely to engage it in more fully.

On the other end of the spectrum is Yolanda, who opts to dispense more cash out of the ATM than to sort through the cash littering her apartment. And while I am here to reorganize her suitcases, I can't resist the urge to manage her assets. Our latest session results in three hundred and forty-seven dollars. She is astonished at how quickly the money added up. I put it into plain terms for her: this money could have been a course in learning Italian or Spanish, two things she wants to do this fall. As it is, most of the money we found today goes toward the hotel bill in Taos. The rest of the cash is for her weekly expenses, which we tuck into a hot-pink crocodile wallet that she loves but has yet to use. When the experience is enjoyable, you are likely to engage it in more fully. Next, we set up the in-store ritual where she places the money back into her wallet before leaving the store — all bills in order, monopoly style. If it helps, I offer, think of me as a child with my brother Matthew building our future fortunes. With a little practice, Yolanda could be placing hotels on Park Place in no time.

THE WAY
Treat your money with respect.

DAILY PRACTICES

✓ Start an in-store ritual where you always place your bills and coins neatly back in your wallet. A good way to respect your money and know what you have at the same time is to place bills in the same direction and in descending denomination. If you have a wallet that is too full with incidentals, take the time this week to organize, purge, and tidy.

✓ Now that your wallet is tidy, take the time to look at your credit cards. Do you have a card for every store? This tendency makes expense tracking harder. Obey the financial rule of two lines of open credit, which is easier to maintain and will keep your credit report organized.

✓ Determine your relationship with money. Do you respect your money or treat it carelessly? Understanding how you value this personal asset is the first step to making your money fuel your dreams.

✓ When possible, make exact change at the store; this will lighten your wallet and help you save even more. If you are a change collector, get a bunch of paper coin rolls to organize your change.

✓ Credit and debit cards often give us a false sense of the value of money. This week, pay cash only, and become more aware of how much you spend each week.

✓ Make a place for coupons and discount cards. If you have them with you, you are more likely to use them — and they represent real money in your pocket.

25

I Am Busier than Thou

IS IT MY imagination, or is everyone in a new competition to see how busy he or she can be? Ask anyone what they've been up to, and the reply is usually, "Oh, I have been busy, busy as a bee, running here and there, can't keep up, there is just so much to do."

Pardon me, but what the heck is everybody busy doing? Arguably, our lives should be getting more efficient with technology, allowing us to do more with less. I rarely hear people make the excuse that they are so busy having fun with friends and family that they have no time to work. And while this seems like a completely modern malady, my forefather in the simplicity movement, Henry David Thoreau, asked the same questions of his peers back in the midnineteenth century. He demanded answers, too. "Busy, busy, busy and so are the bees, but what are we busy doing?" he commented in 1857. And just think, Thoreau completely dropped out of society to escape modern innovations like the battery and the sewing machine. I shudder to think what his reaction would be to the distractions of today. And although completely dropping out of our busy lives is not a reality for most, we can seek answers that allow us to live in this modern world more peaceably by taking a cue from Thoreau, who advocated inner reflection rather than outer stimulus.

Back to his and my earlier question: what is the root of all this busy business? Our modern habits call for "more." We buy more stuff, eat larger portions, drive giant SUVs, and live in bigger homes. As a nation we are addicted to self-improvement — and that usually means adding yet more to our lives: a new diet book, a better computer, a gym membership. But if we focus our thinking to internal needs versus external stimuli, we might find that we don't need as much.

And therein lies the prize, the inner Walden Pond where we focus on our true priorities rather than the business of being busy. We begin to evaluate activities that are important to us rather than joining the busy contest. A good example comes from the very maligned Facebook profile page, which is designed for members to tell everyone what they are doing as if proving our importance. Some good examples come from the most basic and arguably unnecessary entries, like "So tired today after long night out" or "Off to a business meeting." And then there is the bragging post like, "Doing a photo shoot, working, and baking cookies." I was guilty of this one last holiday season. What was I trying to prove? To tell my network about my efforts so they will virtually pat me on the back? And the funny thing about it is that it works. People write nice comments to reward you for being busy, causing the misinterpretation that "busy" means "important."

Further lessons come from my circle of first-time mothers in Hoboken, New Jersey, most of whom left high-

powered careers in Manhattan to become full-time, stay-at-home moms. Yet these mothers are now in a new brand of business — and busyness: attending play dates and music classes, hitting the playground, and on the side keeping up with the laundry, housekeeping, grocery shopping, pediatrician appointments, and feeding. This brand of busyness is one that teaches a valuable life lesson because their new bosses, their babies, do not understand the concept of busy. They don't care if the laundry needs to be folded or if the plumber arrives to fix a leaky faucet or if a former office mate is on the phone. They want you, and they want you *now*. That is what *they* are busy about: loving and being loved. They are not concerned with the busy business of life. They have no agenda.

As grown-ups, of course, we all have agendas — hidden or otherwise. But how we choose to fill our agenda is where we can make the difference and decide how busy we want to be. Mr. Thoreau set his own example by taking off to Walden Pond, but each of us needs to seek our own methods to combat the hectic madness. It begins with evaluating our activities, finding the ones with the most meaning, and pursuing them. And if those things make us busy, perhaps we can be busy in a better way.

THE WAY
Do not rush through your life like it's a series of hurdles with the most frenetic person winning. Pause to evaluate your activities for meaning before writing them into your schedule.

DAILY PRACTICES

✓ Consider a new take on your daily planner by listing the things you are missing out on due to being overbooked, overscheduled, and overstimulated. If some recurrent theme is taking place, like blowing off Spanish lessons or constantly rescheduling the massage, reset your equilibrium to achieve balance by recognizing what those imbalances delay.

✓ Choose that something no longer fulfills you or has lost any meaning. If you have events scheduled that you "should" or "have to" attend, drop one of these from your calendar this week and see what space — and even relief — that provides.

✓ It used to be that we had to find time to motivate ourselves off the couch; now we don't have time to listen to ourselves think. Create a practice of stillness every day to simply meditate on the events of the day. Sitting in stillness helps quiet the mind to create focus and clarity.

✓ Follow the simple rule of finding time for friends, family, and meaningful activities. If most of your time is spent with people who drain your energy, activities that no longer interest you, or commitments born out of obligation only, you may be missing out on more fulfilling experiences. Start with what gives you pleasure first, and build your life around those — the people and activities that enrich you.

✓ Are you addicted to constantly reporting to others what you are doing, when you are doing it, and why? If you spend more time updating your Facebook status page than actually living your life, it is time to be present in your day, not reporting about it.

✓ Turn reporting into accountability, and put technology to work for you. Use social networking facilities like Facebook and Twitter to help propel you forward with a challenge you are working on, such as looking for a service worker, a job, or help with a consumer choice.

I AM IN the midst of teaching a savvy group of media professionals in New York City how to be organized when we come to an exercise that stumps the class. I ask, "What is everybody good at?" No one answers. Part of getting organized and making changes has to do with confidence — the con-

26
Let Go of the Outcome

fidence to move forward to try something new, regardless of how it turns out. The group that I am teaching is lacking this confidence, and I suspect that they are no different from most people. I continue, "What are your personal assets? Can anyone operate a stick shift, bake a pie, or ride a bike?" Still nobody answers.

This is dumbfounding. Perhaps I am egotistical, but I can do a lot; make risotto, put a baby to sleep, and be a good listener are all skills that I am proud of. But this group can't come up with a single skill. I tell them they are all confident, capable individuals because I happen to know that some of them have started their own businesses, graduated with advance degrees, and traveled the world. Yet they are paralyzed when it comes to gaining the confidence they need to make the necessary changes to eliminate their clutter. All those piles of delayed decisions have cluttered their confidence. Learning how to do anything requires a learning curve, a defined period of being a beginner. Those who have changed careers, gone back to school, or written a novel all started with little knowledge and gained experience and skills along the way. Like any other learning process, organizing requires trial and error to figure out what works best.

> Like any other learning process, organizing requires trial and error to figure out what works best.

For some reason a group competent in so many other disciplines needed their organizing confidence boosted. It was worst-case-scenario time. I ask, "What would happen if you were to organize your sock drawer by color and then after two weeks decided that you did not like it? Could you change it?" "Yes," they answer in unison with a chuckle. "How would that make you feel?" I ask, donning my best psychologist voice. "OK," most of them say.

Based on that simple philosophy, if you know how to change something, why not try something different and perhaps better, knowing that if it does not work, you can always change it later? After all, you will be in no worse a situation than you are right now, and you might even be getting closer to your goal. By beginning, you will gain the confidence to make the mistakes and deal with them — just as you have done with every other skill you have mastered in your life.

Suddenly the group is emboldened. They shout out their skills:

"I can run an Excel spreadsheet!"

"I can fly a kite!"

"I can whistle!"

Bravo, class; now you are ready to get organized. After all, you have already taken the first step by enrolling in this class. Pats on the back all the way around!

THE WAY
Being solution-oriented is a good thing; it shows that we have forethought and responsibility for our actions — but focusing too much on the outcome erodes our confidence. Embrace mistakes, and know that you have the ability to deal with any outcome.

DAILY PRACTICES

✓ The first step is the hardest one but a necessary one to make any change. Spend a few minutes as this week begins to describe the fears or hesitations that hold you back from getting started; often we are limited by a false notion of what a job will entail. Recognizing what holds us back is the first step to releasing it.

✓ Embrace your power, and send harmful emotions packing. When we spend too much time thinking about what we don't know, we often lose out on what we can learn. Eliminate negative thinking and adapt to the flow of the world around you. Observe how changing this mind-set opens up a new way of thinking and how trial and error can work in your favor.

✓ Take a confidence reality check. Compare getting organized to any of the other processes in your life, and you will see a common theme: the learning curve. Be emboldened by the process of true self-improvement, and let past successes in other disciplines give you the confidence you need to try something new. Become a natural explorer by collecting new experiences and the knowledge they bring.

✓ Change is a constant in life. Those who readily embrace change build their adaptability muscles. They learn that mistakes are a part of life and are more able to deal with them. Viva la mistake! Know that you have the power to change and adapt to whatever life offers you.

✓ Observe the role control plays in your life. Adopt the attitude that everything will turn out as planned rather than obsessing over the outcome, which may or may not be under your control.

✓ Press the pause button. Often forward thinking propels our minds so far into the future that we cannot embody the present. Eliminate the constant fast forwarding that happens when you think about initiating a project. Concentrate on the joy of the process, and the outcome will take care of itself.

THERE ARE TWO different types of people: bakers and cooks. Bakers adhere to recipes, check for proper ingredients, and carefully follow directions. They rarely improvise. Cooks add a bit of this and a dash of that and often experiment with ingredients and techniques. Bakers are optimists, trusting that if they

27
Create a Life Recipe

do everything according to the recipe, the final product will turn out right. Cooks are cynics, needing more reassurance; they season and taste along the way to make sure there are no surprises.

Personally, I have baker envy. Regardless of my numerous attempts to join this elite group, my baked goods are quite bad. Holiday baking does not pass without frantic phone calls to my baker friend Patricia, who has repeatedly talked me through some tough sugar-cookie recipes. Even my baker mother asks, "Why, with so many good bakeries in your town, would you ever try this at home?" And perhaps the icing on my cake, when going to dinner at friends' homes, is that I always reassure the host that I will bring something — as long as it is not baked.

So why can't I make a decent cake? Baking has rules, a natural order where steps and ingredients are precisely followed to ensure a delicious outcome. This is where I get tripped up. It can be easy to get ahead of oneself in life but not in baking. Betty Crocker is unforgiving. You only need to use salted rather than unsalted butter in a carrot cake recipe once to understand this seemingly innocuous substitution.

Here a valuable lesson can be learned: rushing through the steps leads to mistakes. As evidenced by the countless

cakes that I have tossed directly into the garbage, a case can be made that doing things slowly and correctly the first time has its merits. Focusing on each step is crucial to the process. This painstaking approach teaches the novice baker patience and ultimately confidence. Impatient bakers learn quickly that you cannot fudge a fudge recipe. Believe me, I have tried. Still with so many fallen soufflé setbacks, I want to bake well.

Someone once said that you learn more from failure than success. With that in mind, I hop back into the kitchen for more education as often as possible.

THE WAY

What will be your recipe for life, a slow methodical approach or a taste-and-see one? Knowing your kitchen tactic may provide insight to your life outside the kitchen. Create your own secret recipe, gather all the ingredients, and take it one step at a time.

DAILY PRACTICES

✓ Examine both the cook and the baker to determine what kind of approach you take in life. If your balance shifts from time to time, more consistency might help gain clarity. Realign your day differently by incorporating the opposite approach.

✓ Open yourself up to the idea of thoughtful spontaneity, which may provide an unexpected reward in your life. Achieve a small, unexpected act of pleasure today; call an old colleague to say hello, or listen to a favorite song. Pause and recognize the benefits.

✓ With your new outlook on life, think about the essential ingredients in your recipe. Do you have everything you need to move forward or are you still in need of components? Consider the kinds of activities, hobbies, and even people you would like to enjoy more of this week.

✓ If you have ever had a nagging feeling of something missing, you also know the accompanying discomfort. Take a tip from the Buddhists this week by embracing that discomfort and letting it guide you to great opportunity. Contemplating what is missing in our lives can often point us to getting exactly what we want. Taking time to dance or sketch, engaging in fulfilling conversations, or pursuing a dream career might be what completes your list.

✓ Consider the notion of satisfaction in all aspects of your life: career, family, friends, passions, and hobbies. At times, one ingredient might overpower another. Think about making a balanced plan for life satisfaction by adding a bit of another ingredient. Note this in your weekly routines and habits, and create a combination that suits your taste.

✓ Now that you have identified some of the "keepers" in your life, begin to strike a daily balance that includes all aspects in equal part. When we identify our essentials, we can create a life of our choosing. As Emily Dickinson once said, we can dwell in the possibility.

28

The Way You Do Anything Is the Way You Do Everything

SHELBY IS A motivated self-starter with an incredible attention to detail. She takes her job seriously, is never late for work, and often asks for more responsibility. Her colleague Kristin makes mistakes, is constantly late for work, and often misses deadlines. When asked for status reports, Kristin has multiple excuses and requires constant supervision to complete her daily work. If you needed something done, you obviously would rely on the person you can trust to get the job done. You would turn to Shelby, not Kristin.

We all have a Shelby and a Kristin in our lives. Kristin's cavalier nature is causing her to miss more than just a few deadlines. Her behavior erodes both her productivity and the trust of those around her. This bad habit perpetuates the philosophy that the way you do anything is the way you do everything. Reliability is a cultivated practice that applies to all the tasks in life, big or small. It must be instilled daily to become a good habit that builds character and increases dependability. Reliability is not something that can be turned on and off like a light switch as we choose.

Honoring the task at hand, no matter how small, may be in contrast for many who feel they are too busy to sweat the small stuff. But it is the small stuff that makes up most of what we do on a daily basis — and those little things bolster our ability to handle the big stuff. Without this build, errors occur, leading to a lack of trust and confidence. This resurgence of sweating the small stuff is both Zen and modern at

the same time — Zen in that it asks us to slow down and be more present and modern as it employs the idea of finding more meaning in our lives.

The idea of phoning it in — whether land line or cell — is so yesterday. Trust is the new currency. We should be able to trust our coworkers, our friends and family, and at some level the service people we encounter, from the dry cleaner to a security guard. These relationships all require an unwritten contract of trust, one that, if we honor it, we can better ourselves. And once we better ourselves, we are in an improved position to help others — and that is not only the key to doing things well but also making the world a better place. Holding others to these small social and professional commitments is step one in this universal process.

If Shelby and Kristin were my employees, I would not treat them differently. As their supervisor, I would consider their results objectively, which would mean holding them equally accountable for their actions. This is all logical and doable, but the challenge comes with the "how." A friend once gave me sage advice: you can disagree with someone's ideas, but that does not mean that you have to change your opinion of the person. That is the key in this situation, as well. Letting Kristin know what you think about her work style should not reflect how you feel about her as a person. It is important to separate the two. With this kind of thinking, we all become one another's mentors, where our individual strengths can benefit others. And that is something we all can learn from.

> **THE WAY**
> Holding each other accountable for small actions results in taking pride in our work and in our lives. With this kind of universal approach, you will realize that the way you handle even the smallest situations indicates how you will handle the larger ones too.

DAILY PRACTICES

✓ Consider your reliability factor. Are you a person your friends can rely on? Do you do what you say you will do? Do you keep people waiting or never return phone calls? Address how the small stuff in your life is being neglected, and make a decision to change.

✓ Intention is what you mean to do before you do it. You may have the best intentions, but your actions may not reflect that. If you act with a true heart from the beginning, your intention will shine through. Track your personal trajectory of intention to action.

✓ Do all of your tasks well, no matter how small. Become the "go-to" person whom people can rely on to get things done. Make your personal stamp one of reliability, not excuse making. Record the observations of those around you as you make this subtle shift.

✓ Gandhi counseled, "Be the change you wish in the world." Strive to be the best you can be. Often we talk the talk without walking the walk. This week make those two actions synonymous by setting a shining example.

✓ Authenticity is the key to happiness. Being authentic means acting in a way that is meaningful and truthful to your higher purpose. Consider the role of your authentic self as you move through your week, and make sure that when you perform the everyday activities in your life, they have meaning to you.

✓ Using the guiding words of Gandhi, notice the benefits of holding yourself to a higher standard. When you realize that you are not doing anyone any favors by letting them slide professionally or socially, you can ultimately change your part of the world.

STACEY HAS A dilemma. Her boss is demanding the midyear report three months early on the same day she has a dental appointment for a nagging, lingering toothache. She is in a quandary about what to do. This kind of dilemma happens once in a while to most people when two competing priorities meet up to impose an impossible choice. But for Stacey, these situations render her helpless on a daily basis.

Manage Competing Priorities

Life is full of competing priorities that are at odds with one another because they require the same amount of urgency and importance. But their occurrence should be more of an occasional, not an everyday, thing. When

reviewing Stacey's daily slate of priorities, we can see which hold the same level of urgency and importance and how often these impossible choices derail her life. Here is where a strategic planning mode can put Stacey — and the rest of us — in the driver's seat.

"Strategic planning mode" is priority setting; it allows us to control our priorities and make time for them accordingly. Stacey constantly feels as though all of her priorities are bumping together. Think of it as cars merging into one lane at rush hour. Ultimately, only one can go through at a time, one will always take precedence. The most aggressive driver displays a level of urgency — perhaps the driver is en route to a hot date — and nothing will stand in his way. His level of urgency wins.

Translate all those rush-hour cars jockeying for a position on the on-ramp to life situations that often happen simultaneously. For Stacey, it feels like something either takes precedence over her needs, placing her in the trailing car, or puts her in implementation mode where she scrambles to do things faster, not necessarily better. In this reactive state, also known as fight or flight, the body reacts to stress by producing a hormone known as cortisol. Producing too much cortisol not only flings Stacey out of control on a daily basis but also can lead to serious health issues over time, such as anxiety, depression, and weight gain. Practicing mind over matter is critical.

And if Stacey does not prepare herself to manage her life in a more rational manner, she may be risking more than losing a dental appointment or disappointing her boss.

Stacey remedied her immediate situation with an easy but strategic fix. Before overreacting, she asked her boss to clarify the assignment and his level of urgency. Turns out the project was due by week's end, not day's end. And Stacey had already plugged half the numbers into a new computer system, so she had been prepared after all. She headed off to the dental appointment with a calm confidence, knowing that she had strategically eliminated a competing priority. But this lesson gave her a wake-up call for being more prepared for future scheduling conflicts.

> Life is full of competing priorities that require the same amount of urgency and importance. But their occurrence should be more of an occasional, not an everyday, thing.

THE WAY

Switch gears from implementation mode, where you are adding more and more and have to do things faster, to strategic planning mode, where you approach tasks more methodically and in a smarter way.

DAILY PRACTICES

✓ Recognize the competing priorities in your life and how often they conflict with one another. Determine if these priorities are of the same level of importance and urgency. If you are constantly putting out fires, you are not allotting the proper amount of time for completion of your tasks. Approach this week as a controlled proactive thinker rather than someone who reacts under stress.

✓ Look at your priorities, and rank them in terms of importance, putting the most important on the top. Identify the big goals in your day, and dedicate time to work on those. Note how many big goals you are attacking at once, and readjust your expectations to a more realistic approach.

✓ When we move into panic mode, our minds often focus on the less important. Avoid the flight or fight tendency that can cause unnecessary stress. Be aware of this tendency as you move through your week, and note where a different, more methodical, approach can be employed.

✓ Stress can be addictive; like a drug, it often gives us a rush or even a false sense of importance. Make the distinction this week between creating drama and eliminating drama. This may mean sending your inner diva into the wings.

✓ Do not jump to conclusions without all the facts. Our nature of reaction is a stronger impulse than analytical thought, one that often creates undue stress and pressure. Become a fact finder before making a judgment, and leave emotional impulses at the door.

✓ Stress is a chain reaction that has unhealthy and harmful conclusions. Feeding into this pattern of pressure does much more harm than simply ruining your day. Keep your health in mind when getting worked up over situations that are out of your control. A steady approach will improve your overall well-being.

30

Merge Your Partner

KMART AND SEARS did it, Procter & Gamble did it, and even Hall and Oates did it. So why was it so difficult for my new husband and me to create a merger? In our case, stuff was the issue. We took inventory before we moved into our new apartment. Like Noah loading the ark, we counted up the cargo: two DVD players, two TVs, two microwave ovens, two toasters, and two complete sets of every Van Morrison album ever recorded, my husband's on vinyl and mine, compact disc. Was our stuff more compatible than we thought?

We made a case for each of our possessions — which should be kept and which should be discarded. We bargained over who had the better copy of Bob Dylan's *Blonde on Blonde*, who had the better telephone, and whose comforter was softer. During this process, we realized that other voices demanded notice, most notably those of our past relationships. When leafing through his weathered edition of *The Road Less Traveled*, I noticed the inscription and shouted, "Who the heck is Lindsey?" Our stuff was telling our stories even when we said nothing. At the same time, in an apartment across the Hudson River, my friend Dianna was preparing for a move to the West Coast. While emptying the contents of her New York apartment and her New York life, she found a pair of skis and exclaimed, "Those skis are so three boyfriends ago!"

Whether it's a hardcover book or dusty skis, we hold on to stuff — and some things from our past relationships, too. As if on cue, a choice needed to be made in the middle of my diverging road. The movers arrived with the contents of my husband's bachelor pad, and a 1970s-style papasan chair was suddenly making its way into our new living room. I guess you could say it was the rattan that broke the camel's back. Our possessions summed each of us up in a nutshell. His style was retro fraternity: a collection of every ticket stub to every Grateful Dead show he attended, a ficus tree, a drum set, a box of albums, and a full set of college mugs. The move represented the swan song of his bachelorhood. My style, by contrast, was maximal consumer: 125 pair of shoes, three closets' worth of clothing, and glassware for every cocktail in the bartender's manual. The move represented my preparedness for any situation with the right outfit and appropriate wine glass.

We were faced with the first of many personal challenges as a couple: how to merge the stuff of our individual past lives into our joined future life. Together, we chose the better of the duplicates and had a garage sale with the rest. In the process, we banked a little money for a future home purchase. We compromised, debated, and discussed — and along the way we learned how to make room for each other.

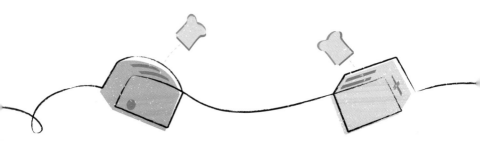

> **THE WAY**
> Help your partner get over separation anxiety by creating a coveted place for all of your mementos, and let the organizing zone be judgment free. Telling your partner that you think his collection of fraternity mugs is ridiculous is the fastest way to have them impede your relationship.

DAILY PRACTICES

✓ Respect and love should be at the center of all communication with your partner. Beginning with the intention of "I love you" will keep you grounded during discussion.

✓ Disagreement in relationships can be difficult, but it does not have to change the way you feel about each other. Be mindful when disagreeing that you deal with the situation, not the person. Making things too personal often leads to hurt feelings. When talking things through, level the playing ground by eliminating emotion.

✓ Living together takes space planning. When moving in with your partner, make sure to carve out space for each of your belongings as well as a space you share together. Cluttering into one another's space will lead directly to conflict, so mark off the real estate.

✓ Be present in this relationship. Elements from past relationships can often impede the present and future of the current relationship. Leave a past relationship in the past where it belongs. That may mean parting with some items or mementos.

✓ Value your partner by respecting the things that he or she derives pleasure from. You are different people with different memories and nostalgia, so if something is very important to your partner, ask why so that you can share in the memory.

✓ Be open and honest about your clutter style. Talk about your preferences for tidying the house, sorting mail, hanging up keys and coats. Respectful language such as "it is important to me to live in a clutter-free kitchen, so please put the dishes in the dishwasher after every meal" or "making my bed each day gives me a peaceful start to the day" are constructive ways to tell your partner how you feel.

31

Traveling Light

MY FAVORITE VACATION spot is St. John, one of the pristine U.S. Virgin Islands. Its breath-taking views, nature preserves, and spectacular beaches are my choice for the perfect vacation: getting back to nature and enjoying the relaxation of doing nothing in a tropical environment. I have been visiting the island for a number of years, and I always think of the things I *don't* need when I pack for the trip.

The first year I brought a large suitcase packed to capacity, including numerous pairs of shoes, among them heels, sandals, flats, and sneakers; countless outfits for going out on

the town; a different bathing suit for every day; and multiple exercise outfits. The next year I hauled a smaller suitcase that had less clothing but still too much for St. John. But I'm learning. Each year I pack less and less. The island is casual. You can wear a nice sundress to even the most formal restaurants — and leave the heels at home; the land is hilly and rustic. Last year I packed a small carry-on bag with two bathing suits (quite sufficient, since I always hand-wash them after the beach anyway), a sundress, a few pairs of shorts, one exercise outfit, a pair of flip-flops, a sarong, and two tank tops. I felt like I could write one of those clever travel pieces about what to pack for a tropical vacation.

But beyond my suitcase, St. John itself is low on clutter. There is no shopping mall to stock up on needless items as in the States. And because you have to ferry everything over, including your car, you need to be choosy about what you want to carry. With all that natural beauty, you really don't need anything but a Bob Marley CD as background. I even question the necessity of taking a laptop to the island. The breathtaking views are distraction enough. At this point St. John still lacks traffic lights and a movie theater. It is the simple life with the simple joys of nature that bring me back every year.

This kind of vacation recharger provides the necessary extreme counterbalance to a world of distraction, an antidote that better prepares me to deal with my world from a calm state. In times of high stress, I recall floating on crystal blue water at Cinnamon Beach and staring at the plentiful palm trees that cover the mountains. The breeze of the trees, the warmth of the sun, and the soothing motion of the Caribbean restore my serenity. This memory is my screensaver, a constant reminder of a carefree time without any clutter.

> **THE WAY**
> A vacation is a great way to re-energize your life. Getting away provides needed perspective of another way to live that makes you appreciate your life that much more.

DAILY PRACTICES

✓ When was the last time you planned an escape from your everyday life? If you have never traveled solo, now may be the time for a quiet retreat. If you are feeling the burnout or grind of your daily routine, consider a vacation of solitude to recharge your batteries.

✓ At many yoga studios and retreats, the practice of silence is used for its restorative and beneficial healing properties. Think about including thoughtful solitude in your next getaway, and open your mind to the clarity that quieting the mind can bring.

✓ Create a space in your home for a daily retreat, using a favorite reading chair, a photo of a vacation spot, or a scented candle to spark relaxing memories in the midst of your daily routine.

✓ When you pack for a trip, bring only the most essential and most used items. Carrying heavy baggage has a psychological effect on travel, so travel light — literally.

✓ Practice good travel tips when getting on the road by using multitasking pieces. Use a small clutch that can double as a makeup bag. Wear your workout shoes on the plane. A pashmina can be used as an evening wrap, a sarong, and an airplane blanket. Employing the rule of at least two uses per item will not only keep your suitcase light but also guarantee that you'll use what you pack.

√ In the immortal words of the band Kansas, "Carry on my wayward son." With the new airport restrictions, it rarely makes sense to check luggage, so get those tiny refillable bottles for your favorite liquid products, and purchase a wheeled light suitcase small enough for the overhead compartment. This will help you get to your destination faster and with less stress.

DEBRA AND JACLYN have been friends for years. They were BFFs way before the term became omnipresent in everyday vocabulary. Jaclyn would call Debra for any cir-cumstance, at any time day or night, for any reason. They shared the same town, the same

32

That's What Friends Are For

interests, and even the same clothes. Jaclyn had become dependent on Debra's advice for any situation, big or small. When Debra started dating Paul, something changed. Paul's time with Debra cut into Jaclyn's time, and she did not like it. Inevitably, the relationship changed. Paul had become Debra's priority, her new BFF.

Sometimes it happens that way; we have a gal or guy pal who ushers us into our adulthood — a drinking buddy, a shopping buddy, a confidant. It works for a while when everyone is on a par: single and unattached. When the soul mate enters the picture, the BFF inevitably takes a number two position, which can be unfamiliar.

After a six-month courtship, Paul proposed marriage and a move to San Francisco for him and Debra. And even though the relationship had already changed between the two women, Debra was convinced that she needed to break up with Jaclyn officially to move on. They attempted the "RDT" (relationship defining talk) — the use of an acronym being another sign that there was trouble. The RDT is usually reserved for couples and signals that the apparent soul mates may actually be traveling on divergent life paths. Such questions as, "Where is this relationship going?" are usually followed by the words, "We have to talk." This phrase is often the precursor to a relationship ultimatum — yet another bad idea.

> When circumstances alter a relationship, it can be hard to see whether or not it has a future.

Jaclyn threw down the gauntlet during their talk by forcing Debra to choose between her and Paul. And matters worsened. Jaclyn began to call more often and became hostile when Debra screened her calls. Soon after, the couple made their move to San Francisco, creating a significant physical and mental distance. They had their first child just a year later and are now a busy family of three. Jaclyn, meanwhile, is in the same place — same job and apartment — and is noticeably hostile whenever Debra finds the time in her busy schedule to call her. The two friends have changed and, obviously, so has their relationship.

When circumstances alter a relationship, it can be hard to see whether or not it has a future. Debra recently returned home to visit family and went to see Jaclyn. They had a brief visit, but Debra's focus is now her one-year-old daughter. And while the affection between the friends still exists, their circumstances demand a new chapter for the once BFFs. Two weeks after the visit, Jaclyn called Debra to tell her the difficulties she was having with her new boyfriend, and once again they found common ground. Debra provided the shoulder to cry on at a time of need.

Although their relationship has changed, the two still share genuine affection for each other — and *that* will never change. The ladies have eased into a different stage in their relationship, adopting a more fluid approach. They understand that friends flow in and out, but true friends are always there when you need them most.

THE WAY
Understanding that relationships should evolve with us as we grow is the basis for real connection. If circumstances change to alter the quality of your relationships, accept them as necessary to growth.

DAILY PRACTICES

✓ If a relationship has become burdensome and the conversations tense, it might be time for a thoughtful discussion. People and situations evolve, but a true friend remains constant through all life's challenges.

✓ It is OK to take a break from a relationship that is one sided or taxing. Creating space can often make you appreciate the person and value the friendship more — and create a new way to communicate.

✓ When a significant other comes into your friend's life, understand that you are not being replaced, but an important change has occurred. Giving that person room to explore this newfound love will cement your bond with your friend and enable everyone to be happy.

✓ Treasure the past in your relationships while understanding that anything that goes the long haul needs to evolve with time. Mature your relationships with your maturing lifestyle, and maintain friendships for life by not putting past expectations on future relationships.

✓ Evaluate your ability to be a good friend. Are you a good listener, a shoulder to cry on, someone who can be relied on when the going gets tough? Maintain the quality of your friendships by giving what you hope to receive.

✓ Letting go of relationships that no longer fulfill you is essential to your evolution. Practice the art of civility, and let people make a graceful exit from your life when necessary.

IF YOU CONSISTENTLY put things back where they belong, you will never question where they are. They will always be where you left them. Just like on *Sesame Street,* when the Muppets sing, "One of these things is not like the other. One of these things just doesn't belong. . . ." This lesson is simple enough for a child

33

Propasana, or Everything in Its Proper Place

to master, and there is a reason for that. Think about how many times a day you search for your keys, your wallet, or your coat. What you have really done is put things with other things that don't belong together. If you were to have a logical place for these things, these searches would be eliminated.

In Hindu philosophy, this proper placement is aptly called *propasana.* Take the time to practice propasana so that you don't have to question where your things are. They will be where you expect them to be. My client work capitalizes on these easy methods that appeal to our logic and the way we naturally do things. But if these things are so simple, why are they so hard to do? Like placing the dishes near the dishwasher, not in it. Certainly the effort is not the few seconds it takes to put the dishes inside the dishwasher. Thinking about this task allows us to get off the hook, momentarily, with less work. We convince ourselves that we are saving time, but we are not. I instruct my clients to take these extra seconds to complete the task. Practice this, and you will get better at it.

Establish a "Honey, I'm home" ritual. When you walk in the front door and unload all of your gear of the day, make it easy for yourself by creating a space in the hallway to hang your coat, keys, and electronic devices. These little fixes take just seconds yet make things easier for us in the long run and reinforce the rule of doing, not thinking. Practice this ritual, and over time you will relieve stress and anxiety because you know where everything is.

Disarray comes from taking daily shortcuts because we convince ourselves that propasana takes more effort. Anyone who reaches a Friday after a hectic workweek knows that, once the weekend comes, she does not want to spend it sorting through the laundry and dry cleaning that was haphazardly tossed on the bed, armchair, or closet floor. Avoid these piles with a little daily maintenance and employing the *Sesame Street* lessons of putting similar things together and then putting things back.

Often people try to reinvent the wheel and avoid using things designed for a specific purpose, like a dresser — perhaps the most useful furniture item ever invented. I am constantly surprised by how many people choose to house their lingerie, sweatpants, and sweaters in a variety of bins, baskets, and storage boxes all over the house — sometimes not even in the bedroom, where people naturally get dressed. Ingenuity can be good, but some tried-and-true methods are still the best. Use the rooms of the house as a guide to where things belong. The dining-room table is often an easy target: a large, flat surface where mail always seems to pile up. Soon dry cleaning, keys, coats, and children's schoolwork join the party. Treadmills as external closets, chairs as drawers, and laundry baskets as inboxes come next — and suddenly nothing is used for its original intent.

Instead, respect each item for its express purpose, and create zones within the house. You can avoid the constant resorting that exists when "one of these things is not like

the other." Get the entire family in on this project. Creating a proper place for everyone's things will make organizing easier. After all, it is proper for all people to take control of all their things to practice propasana.

> **THE WAY**
> Think of life as an airplane flight, where everything is returned to its proper place before landing. Practicing consistent propasana will help you land on your feet on a daily basis.

DAILY PRACTICES

✓ Take a house tour with pad and paper, and write down where your items live. If too many unlike things are coexisting, you may have trouble locating them on a continuous basis. Create zones and categories for your items that make sense to you.

✓ Are you missing an obvious piece of furniture that will make finding things easier? Furniture has a specific purpose. Dressers, filing cabinets, and end tables are reliable places for storage. Resist the temptation to reinvent the wheel for these housing essentials.

✓ Zoning your house will help you stay ahead of clutter. Unnatural habits like using kitchen cabinets for shoes or dining-room tables as mailboxes create constant resorting and the risk of misplacing items. Instead, make these big decisions ahead of time, to avoid weekly pileups and confusion.

✓ Consider how many times you misplace frequently used items and how much time you regularly lose searching for them. This week come up with logical places to house your most-used essentials, whether it's a bowl for keys in the front foyer, a hook for your hat and coat, or a basket for newspapers and magazines.

✓ Recognize the favorites in your life and how easy it is to find them. The things you use most often should have the prime real estate. If they don't, change that now.

✓ Practice propasana every day by putting things back immediately after use. A few seconds now will save you hours later.

34

Choosing
Sophie

HOBOKEN, NEW JERSEY, is a mile-square posh enclave just across the Hudson River from Manhattan. The town is made up predominantly of post-college professionals who settle in for a few years before settling down with a family and a yard in the suburbs. At least that was the case for my peer group and me when we moved here in 1992. Now that I'm married with children, it seems to me that the town is evolving with its aging demographic. Instead of moving to the suburbs like our predecessors, we are sticking around. Where once stood notorious saloons where unsuspecting men were "shanghaied" to work on freighters, baby-gear stores and daycare centers now stand.

Hoboken has morphed from its blue-collar past. But one thing that has not changed is how the residents influence each other, much as they did to buy stirrup pants and mane combs back in the '80s. The new brand of peer pressure is the baby accessory. Hoboken, unlike most other New Jersey towns, is a walking town. Your stroller is like your car, so what kind you have says a lot about you. Personally, I have a deluxe jogging stroller because maneuverability is my primary requirement. When I was still in the market for one, I considered the Stoke stroller, which looks more like a state-of-the-art luge than a baby carriage. But when offered this must-have stroller for $1,500, I told the salesperson that my Honda Civic had cost only three times that price. The logic of plunking down that much money for a state-of-the-art *anything* but especially a stroller seemed a little ridiculous. Oscar Wilde once said that temptation was the only thing he could not resist. I can relate.

While I was patting myself on the back for resisting that temptation, another one — albeit a far-less-expensive one — snuck in. I had noticed that in my baby's peer group, the little ones were all gumming the same toy, a small, squishy, odd-looking giraffe named Sophie. She was French, but her streamlined plastic body was manufactured in Israel, where apparently no harmful additives or dyes are added to children's toys. (When we grew up, we were likely eating lead-based paints and inhaling asbestos but, hey, we turned out OK, despite not having the safety measures now afforded our children.)

"You simply must have it," the salesperson insisted. To be honest, I was feeling a little pressure to buy *something*

after rebuffing the expensive stroller and thought, how much could a little teether cost? A few dollars seemed reasonable for that Israeli ingenuity and the comfort of knowing that other mothers would see that I, too, had made the Sophie choice. I agreed to the purchase.

"That will be $22, please."

"For a *teether?!*" I blurted out.

The salesperson told me that Sophie is never discounted, and if I were to walk down the street to the next kids' shop, *she* would cost *more* there — should they even have any left. Who could argue with that logic? I love to get things for less, so I buy *her*. I quickly unwrap Sophie for little Matthew, hoping that he will love her like all the other babies do, even though his toy track record has not been great. In fact, he could not care less about toys, preferring my cell phone (which I probably should not give him but do), the remote control (the last time he played with it, he turned the entire TV screen pink), and my husband's sunglass case (which is a hazard to anyone who puts their fingers near the latch). He had seemed to like Sophie in the store, but once at home, he showed no interest. I should have put those $22 in his polka-dot piggy bank. On a trip to the park just a few days later, Sophie disappeared — of all toys to go, it had to be the most expensive if not the most coveted. In an instant, she was gone, and I wondered if she was ever really ours to begin with.

THE WAY
Resist putting your money where your good intentions are. Being influenced by peers can often help you make an informed decision, but keeping up with the Joneses for appearance's sake often results in empty purchases.

DAILY PRACTICES

✓ Your peers influence your decisions, so be thoughtful about soliciting advice and knowledge. Often we are unconsciously led to keeping up with those around us whether we realize it or not. Notice how much you are following and how much you are leading.

✓ Saying no is one of the hardest challenges in life. This week practice saying "no, thank you" gracefully, and resist the urge to spend — even when a pleasant and knowledgeable salesperson is guiding your shopping trip.

✓ Release the idea of emotional buying from your world. Make better shopping choices by finding out the best product for your needs, price point, and usage. Just because everyone has the latest state-of-the-art gizmo does not mean that it will work for you.

✓ Returning items is a time-wasting pursuit. If your impulse buying is requiring constant trips back to the store, you are buying too quickly without the proper research.

✓ Do not discount the idea of window-shopping. The art of shopping around is a refined skill whereby you can find the best bargains, wait for a sale, and, most importantly, purchase when you actually need something.

✓ Bail on the sale — don't fall victim to buying something just because it is discounted. Our temptation to stockpile and save often spurs bulk purchasing of unneeded items. Appreciate abundance while knowing that you can always get more.

35

Communication Breakdown

MY ELEVEN-YEAR-OLD nephew Nicholas wants a cell phone. He does his homework on a computer; he surfs online for information to do a book report, he has a gaming device, and he's the only one in his family who can set up Rock Band so that all the instruments can be heard. His childhood is very different from mine.

He is a gamer; I did not even have Atari pong. (My great pleasure was going to the library every Saturday to check out Laura Ingalls Wilder and Judy Blume books.) My rotary phone usage (cell phones were unheard of) was limited; he wants a cell phone so he can Tweet his cell-phone-owning friends. (I thought only birds tweeted.) He has a Wii; we played Trivial Pursuit on a well-weathered game board with plastic chips and wheels and dice. He has an iPod; I had vinyl records. He DVRs; I watched the first run of *The*

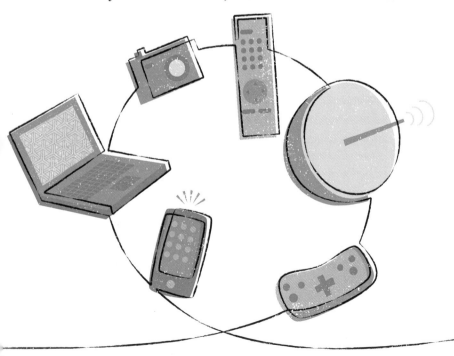

Brady Bunch. He gets instant photos with a digital camera; I went to Fotomat to get prints. He uses a remote control; I *was* the remote control when my dad wanted to change stations. He has a satellite dish that beams in hundreds of channels; my family's TV had rabbit ears that picked up the big-three networks.

In many ways Nicholas will have an easier life with many more conveniences, which is the goal of all technology. I think about this at a Super Bowl party with my good friends. As I head to the bedroom to store my coat, a woman is on her cell phone with a client. She hangs up and exclaims, "Why is this client calling me at 7 p.m. on Sunday night?! Doesn't she realize I have something better to do?" I, of course, cannot resist pointing out, "Well, she probably thinks you have nothing better to do because you answered the phone."

> We have come very far very fast, and all the technological advances can be tempting. To truly harness technology's power is to control its grip on you.

I am never one to pass up a teaching moment — and the two Rum Runner cocktails I've had erased any inhibitions I might have had about speaking up. (Rum Runners are an intelligence tonic, and drinking them has only increased my wisdom.) "You see, when you make yourself available all the time to everyone, they expect you to pick up any time, anywhere. So in essence you created that behavior," I instruct. What I am trying to impart to this tech junkie is that technology is a tool we can access or not access as we choose. She is apparently dumbfounded by my slightly preachy sermon. (Perhaps she has not tried the Rum Runners?) She nods distractedly and seems a bit off balance as she leaves the bedroom. I, too, am pondering, thinking about little Nicholas and his desire for a cell phone. If he does get one, I hope that he has the ability to set boundaries for turning it off and on.

As I prepare a bit more wisdom juice, I am comforted by the fact that technology will not be the kind of novelty in his life as it is mine. Technology for my rabbit-ears generation is still awe-inspiring compared to Nicholas's earbud generation. We have come very far very fast, and all the technological advances can be tempting. To truly harness technology's power is to control its grip on you. Like any vice (Rum Runners included), we choose our entry point and availability. We just have to be careful not to lose our humanity in the process.

> **THE WAY**
> Technology exists to help humans, not vice versa.

DAILY PRACTICES

✓ With so many technological must-haves out there for virtually everything, it can be daunting to figure out what is right for you. Make a list of what you actually need, and then find a piece of equipment that fulfills those needs, not vice versa.

✓ We often get short-circuited from too many outside stimuli. This week create a technology-free zone for one hour a day. Make your walk, car ride, or commute home a hiatus from technology. Choose noninterference, and enjoy focusing and regrouping without pesky interruption.

✓ Do you have technology boundaries? Or do you cringe yet answer anytime, anywhere when your cell phone rings? Remember that you choose how available you want to be, so set boundaries and space for phone, e-mail, and texting. Turn off your phone at inopportune times, and let the messages go to voicemail.

✓ Set parameters for children's technological usage. As a parent, one of the hardest things to do is say no. If keeping up with the other kids is the sole motivation for purchasing unnecessary technology, take a break and communicate the rules that work for your family.

✓ Computers are great at multitasking, but humans are not as good. Note the role of multitasking with your technology this week, and see if you can limit your focus to doing one thing at a time — or at least using one device at a time.

✓ Tune in, not out. While technology helps us to keep in touch with more friends and family more easily than we ever did before, it can also tune us out to what is going on in the world right around us. Be mindful of tuning in to your surroundings. Human interaction is an essential part of our experience, so don't shortchange yourself by plugging in a device rather than talking to another person.

36

Committee Meeting

IN THE LATE 1990s, a TV show called *Herman's Head* depicted different people acting out the emotions of the main character, Herman. Each represented a different part of his personality — sensitivity, anger, intellect, and lust, to name a few. I sympathized with Herman. He was constantly trying to make every one of those voices in his head happy. He tried to take the lead among these equal and important parts, which was the premise of the show's conflict and one that plays out in our daily lives, too.

Decisions by committee inherently have no leader; rather, a group of equally subordinate voices seek to find common ground. Psychoanalysts Sigmund Freud and Eric Berne both identified different aspects of the psyche as roles that we take part in — parent, adult, child personalities according to Berne's theory; id, ego, and superego states in Freud's. (My committee often includes a dozen voices clamoring for the floor.)

Picturing these divergent voices and opinions as a group trying to reach consensus sheds light on why decision making can take so long and be so difficult. At any given time an emotional member may tell you that even though your husband did not mean to hurt your feelings when he told you that you needed a haircut, you can't help but feel hurt — while a more practical member takes your husband's side, agreeing that you are ready for a trim. Or the child member

in us acts up when a huge work assignment is heaped on our desk last minute, and we stomp our feet. At times one voice might overpower the others, similar to the process we go through when we coordinate with coworkers, team members, family, and friends.

This kind of brain clutter can interfere with how we make judgments and move forward with our tasks and at times may even hinder our relationships. It begs the question, who is in charge up there? All this brain clutter needs to be cleared, like files on our desk or dishes in the sink. My favorite story comes from Patty, a mother of three. For a school project, her daughter was asked to present a theoretical gift to each of her parents. The child chose a golf vacation for her father; for her mother she chose "just five minutes to herself." From the mouths of babes came a request for a committee recess, a cease fire. Patty exemplifies how much static we have in our attic.

I ponder this while I get my husband-suggested haircut. (As the director of the committee, I finally led my group to the right decision.) My stylist asks if I want something to read while my hair dries, and I quickly reply, "No. I am fine here alone with my thoughts." We all need time away to corral the inner voices, regardless of what roles they perform. Understanding the different aspects of our personality and the important roles they play help us to achieve a balanced psyche. As in any group dynamic, it is important to give each member a voice, but don't let any one voice overpower them all.

THE WAY
Taking time for reflection and solitude can help you voice your concerns internally, which will enable you to come to a consensus about what is right for you.

DAILY PRACTICES

✓ Quieting the mind is an important step in our self-control. Once this is mastered, we become better able to deal with any situation that comes our way. Experiment with a meditation CD or DVD this week to help guide you through this ancient practice.

✓ In the comedy *What About Bob?*, Bill Murray's character's well-known line is, "Take a vacation from your problems." He simply puts them out of his mind temporarily. At times we belabor a situation only to keep coming up with the same frustrating solution. Today, identify a nagging problem and make a conscious effort to put it aside for a few hours. Revisit it when you have had ample time away.

✓ Take a deep breath. If you consistently find yourself frustrated and anxious, calm your body physically with 10 deep inhalations. Your mind will follow suit as the cleansing oxygen pumps into your body. Picture breathing good thoughts in and bad thoughts out.

✓ If you have never done journal writing, now might be the time to start. Recording your thoughts and observations can often shed new light on familiar situations that only reside in your head. It need not be formal; you can simply list the pros and cons of a challenge or situation you are struggling with.

✓ According to psychologists, our committee defines the complex parts of our personality. It is important to give voice to all these facets, but be careful when the infighting leads you to a frustrating solution. Take the time to listen and balance the divergent parts of your mind to achieve a solution that is right for all aspects of your persona.

✓ A mantra is an inspirational message that is repeated daily to relax and quiet the mind. Create a personal mantra, and lead your inner committee to join in on the chorus.

WOULD I RATHER be right or be happy? This is a question I often ponder, especially when I am in the midst of those pesky life moments that I know I should walk away from but don't. Let me illustrate an example of the daily annoyances that can derail my otherwise benevolent mood. At the checkout

37

Be Happy, Not Right

line at the supermarket, the person in front of me — who is apparently making macaroni and cheese — has neglected to pick up the cheese. He asks if I would mind holding his place in line while he grabs a chunk of cheddar. I say yes, even though this challenges my sense of rule following. More importantly, I ask myself, how did he forget the cheese in the first place? But I digress.

My grocery shopping done, I hop in my car with my righteous meter ticking as if I have sacrificed my first "right" of the day. I find little comfort in knowing that I made him happy. In the parking lot a man cuts me off to maneuver his large truck into the spot reserved for expectant mothers. I refrain

from honking; instead I register another degree on my righteous meter. What is wrong with people today?!

The day ends with a much-deserved coffee break with a friend, to be followed by a leisurely stroll through town. The coffee shop is small, but it is also empty of customers at the moment, so my friend Juli and I roll our strollers in, thinking that it won't take long to grab a cup to go. Even so, the owner of the café is not happy that we have temporarily blocked the entrance. He demands that we move the strollers *immediately.* I react to his anger and hurriedly grumble, "We're leaving, we're leaving" — as if our quick exit will extinguish his unnecessary vitriol. I don't have time to correct him or to argue, so I take the path of least resistance. The sooner we leave, the sooner we put this unpleasantness behind us. I had chosen this place based on its outstanding coffee, and now I feel like I have caused a wrinkle in our otherwise happy afternoon. Juli, on the other hand, has hit full tilt on her righteous meter. She shames the rude owner with kindness, pleasantly explaining that he could have asked nicely and had the same result.

And then the change happens; the owner abruptly apologizes. Juli's example proves that you can have both. She pointed out to the owner that he was wrong, but she did it in a happy way. What a revelation.

It was back in college that I first heard the would-you-rather-be-right-than-happy question posed. At that time most students chose being right, thinking that having both was impossible. When I was younger I made the conscious choice to be right; as I got older, I switched to be happy. It turns out you can be right and you can be happy if you handle things positively and not let anger take over. In fact, you can be right, happy, and enjoy a latte to boot. Who says you can't have it all?

THE WAY
Choosing how to handle a combustible situation is in your hands. We lash out when we let negative emotions take over our feeling of being right. Instead, maintain your position and don't give in to hateful emotions. Following the path of least resistance often causes pent-up emotion, so lead with your heart as well as your head to strike a chord between right and happy.

DAILY PRACTICES

✓ If your righteous meter is constantly ticking, you may need to rethink your approach to matters. Finding new ways to correct a situation can diffuse a volatile situation, so search for constructive methods to get your point across, and lose the stress that accompanies always being right. No one is right all the time, but you can choose to be happy most of the time.

✓ Frequent disagreements with the same people cause an outpouring of anger and emotion that can stand in the way of real problem solving. Instead, agree to disagree, and respect where the other person is coming from. Don't mistake a position on an argument for an opinion about another person. Work this week to separate the two.

✓ The popular movie *Pay It Forward* highlights the idea of acting with kindness in turn when kindness is bestowed on you. Start the kindness cycle by making a conscious effort to help others this week. Begin with one kind act per day.

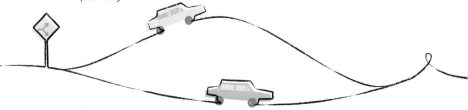

✓ What importance does right represent in your life? Being right is inherent in our makeup, our family influences, and even in our culture. If you are constantly choosing sides to determine blame, consider letting this judgmental approach go this week and observe as a nonjudging bystander.

✓ Being right often goes hand in hand with finding fault. When we make this the barometer for happiness, we erode our own ability to find compassion and practice kindness. It then has the converse affect: we do not become happy, either. Ask yourself if you have ever felt happy about an unkind word spoken. Chances are you always feel happier about choosing the high road of compassion.

✓ There are more ways than one to be right about something. Consider the other viewpoint as valid, too, and you might find that most arguments have more than one side. Usually the truth lies somewhere in the middle, so be willing to meet halfway.

THERE IS AN inherent high when you get something for nothing: a discounted item you thought was full price is on sale, a bartender comps you a martini, or a free lipstick is included with the pressed powder you just bought. There is something wonderful about the

38

Freecycling

gift-with-purchase notion. The last time I did a garage sale, a bargain hunter asked me to throw in a pair of Sony Walkman headphones with the purchase of two ice-cube trays. He was persuasive and bold, and I wanted to make a two-dollar deal. "Ask and it shall be received" works at most places. And with the proliferation of Yahoo groups, Craigslist, and now Freecycle, giving stuff away has never been easier or more expected.

Free can indeed be better — but only when the free item is actually used. Otherwise free can be problematic. Never has this philosophy come to mind more than when I am working in the home of a client who is a beauty magazine editor. She constantly gets freebies: shampoo, deodorant, powder blush, hair thickener, and whitening toothpaste. At black-tie formals goody bags of products are heaped on her, vying for her attention and review. She scoops up armloads of swag, thinking she will pass the items on to someone who can use them. But she is never diligent about doing this, so the piles grow and grow. What remains is a mountain of stuff that no one is using.

Another example of free overload comes from an antiques junkie who picks up castoff dressers, side tables, and armoires that he finds on the street. He can't help but take these pieces home to his cramped apartment, feeling as if he has won a prize. I call this junk transference, where the taker of the item turns a discard into pure euphoria.

We need to resist the urge to collect for the sake of collecting; reject and look at value and usage to guide acquisitions. One might think that because the item was free, you have nothing to lose by picking it up, but the opposite is true: if you have no use for the item, don't crowd your house with it.

> ## THE WAY
> Being addicted to the idea of acquiring something just because it is free misses the point of value. Things are of value only when you use them, not simply because they cost you nothing.

DAILY PRACTICES

✓ Examine the mystique of free. Do you buy something simply because it has a gift with purchase or take friends' castoffs simply because they are without cost? Look at the things you use most. They are probably items you researched and thought through, not ones that you purchased impulsively. That link makes the item more usable because you consciously chose them.

✓ Goody bags and giveaways are tempting, but they rarely contain what we need. This week practice your ability to say no to the unnecessary freebie whether it's an additional credit card, a free lipstick with purchase, or even a free bag of chips with your sandwich. These subtle practices will train you to say no to bigger things.

✓ Establish your need for an item before acquiring it. A good way to see if you are collecting for the sake of collecting is if multiples — say, two desks or two dressers — crowd your house. We often pick things up and find a need for them later when the opposite should be your guiding principle.

✓ Free means free of charge, but that does not mean it is free of space. Something may be costing you space even though it did not cost you money. Seek to create even more space by letting go of something you have held on to simply because it was free.

✓ Free is a new currency in our society, making us devalue things that we have normally paid for in the past — like wireless access, for example. When examining the relationship between "free" and "necessity," ask yourself if the free service is better than one you would happily pay for. At times the abundance of free only delays inherent needs to find and buy what you will use.

✓ Be leery of sales promotions. A good example is computer printers. You may be offered a free printer, and then find that the toner cartridges are very expensive — and are where the retailer makes the real money. Hidden costs down the road can turn the bargain of the century into a money pit.

39

Gossip Gal

THE SCENE IS a familiar one to anybody who watches television or follows the headlines. A clean-cut public figure in a conservative navy suit approaches a bank of microphones as cameras roll. We know he is joining the ranks of public figures who have betrayed their wives, their families, their fans, and their morals. An air of defeat has replaced his signature charisma and self-confidence. The audience salivates. Cameras flash. This man is clearly remorseful and ready to ask the media and the viewing audience for forgiveness for his sins. Because we have seen a similar scenario countless times, the impact of his speech is somewhat diminished.

In recent years, a parade of governors, senators, athletes, and celebrities has adopted this same "make good" speech, which includes nothing new, nothing unexpected. Yet we are as transfixed by the image on the screen today as we were in 1998, when President Clinton admitted his indiscretions. Even so, we know that these public figures are going through the motions, delivering well-written and well-practiced words that have been crafted for them by PR coaches who have had plenty of practice in damage control. These speeches always include just the right balance of remorse and humility.

Once this necessary hurdle is reached, the fallen figure can move on to the next stage: the rise from the ashes. Ratings will climb for that, as well, whether it's Oprah, Jay Leno, or Barbara Walters asking the questions. And

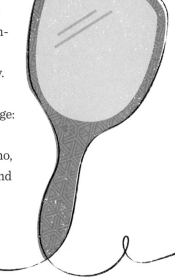

though the scene periodically repeats itself, those addicted to gossip sit front row to bask in another's misfortune. I find this part more fascinating. Perhaps the lives of these celebrities tell us about ourselves more than they do about the celebrity du jour. It can't be that we simply need something else to talk about at the office on Monday mornings.

I ask a good friend, who is a self-admitted gossip maven, why she loves watching the shows and following the tabloids. She tells me this guilty pleasure is one that she just cannot get enough of. When I ask her what she gets out of it, she says relief that her life is not that screwed up. This strikes me as a circuitous route to well-being, but I am willing to play along. I don my best Buddha-enlightened self and probe further. "What does Octomom really have to do with us?" I ask, referencing a recent tabloid sensation. My friend says, "Nothing. That's the point — and it helps me escape from my real life."

Finding the middle ground between Buddha and Gossip Gal is not easy. Gossip shifts our focus from our issues to someone else's and can give us a false sense of superiority — something that Gossip Gal has a good dose of, she tells me proudly. Buddha might say that is the real problem. Our goal should be to focus internally, not externally. Just think of the time we waste watching these carefully controlled press conferences that we could be using for self-improvement. And this is the answer I provide to my gossip girlfriend. When we consciously make that shift, we can eliminate our need to watch all together. Otherwise, as long as we are part of that audience, the media will continue to serve it up.

THE WAY
Look inward at your own life rather than examining the lives of others.

DAILY PRACTICES

✓ Gossip is a temptation that creeps into nearly every aspect of our life: family, workplace, marriage, even our leisure time with friends. Examine your use of gossip about other people and their affairs. If this casual talk involves comments you would never say to someone's face, it is time to take a break.

✓ Inherent in gossip is the ability to harm or defame. As you casually reference others, realize if any of these comments are as playful as you intend them to be. Consider the consequences of your words, and realign your language to be positive.

✓ Talking behind people's backs is a common trait for high-school kids, where jealousy and competition reign supreme. But jealousy and competition also play a role in your adult life and can be strong motivators for gossip. Have you broken your high-school gossip habit, or are you fostering a new clique of gossipmongers?

✓ Lose the tabloids. If *Gawker* and the *National Enquirer* absorb your personal reading time, take a break this week to read something uplifting. Break the cycle of mindless reading, and replace it with something mindful and inspiring.

✓ Consider what saying something about someone else says about you. If you have become either the go-to person for the latest scoop or the person who cannot keep a secret, backtrack and look at your own image. Remember that gossip works both ways.

✓ Consider your relationships with those whom you gossip with. Remember that if it's easy for them to gossip to you, it's just as likely that those people will also gossip about you.

BIBLIOPHILES ARE INTERESTING people. They find the written word so powerful that they cannot let go of books they have loved and even books that they think they *will* love. Unsurprising, then, that in the course of my work, I have found one of the top cluttered

40
Book Keeping

spaces is the bookcase, and one of the top things to store is a book. There are two reasons people keep books: they have read them and think they will read them again, or they plan to read them someday. Either way, people have a difficult time letting books go. It's as if they are waiting for that day when they have so much spare time, they will read several books a day — a scenario that rarely presents itself, unless it's part of a strong fantasy life like mine.

Whenever I watch *The Shawshank Redemption* or come across one of the endless programs about people who are incarcerated, I envision myself in prison, where long days and nights allow me to read nonstop. My actual free life does not allow me to sit and read *The Golden Notebook* from cover to cover, but in the fantasy there are no distractions — no work, iPod, TV, children, husband, or friends to demand my time. I have nothing but time, and nothing but books, so I

devour my "must-read pile" and find that I want more and more to read.

This fantasy, extreme though it may be, is one that we bibliophiles all have versions of. Why else would we buy such 1,000-page tomes as *Gravity's Rainbow* or *Infinite Jest* if we didn't think that someday we will actually have the time to conquer them? Reading is aspirational as well as inspirational, and if not managed like every other organizing project, it can become clutter central.

Personally, I love to pass books on because I not only like to read them, but I like to talk about them, so often keeping them to myself seems unfair. There is no shortage of books, so why not share the wealth? I trust that books will come in and out, confident that there will always be something to read, which is why I thought keeping books was a silly idea — until I met a particular bibliophile best classified

> There are two reasons people keep books: they have read them and think they will read them again, or they plan to read them someday.

as a "rereader." This, of course, flies in the face of my prison fantasy. Read a book twice? I can't even get around to reading some once (excluding my compulsion to reread the travels of Jamie and Claire Fraser in Diana Gabaldon's neverending Outlander series.) The rereader explained that she might pick up *Pride and Prejudice* to reread a Mr. Darcy quote, or she might reread a particular passage that moved her in a work by Henry James. I certainly could not argue with that. Austen's and other classics (or in my case, Diana Gabaldon's books) that are truly loved should be coveted and referenced often.

And of course, exceptions are to be made for the signed and rare, like my complete collection of John Irving first-edition hardcovers, which are behind glass and rarely touched. Before going to my special shelves, my husband often asks if he can actually read one of my books. Many times, the answer is surprisingly, "Of course not! That's a first edition, you silly man!" But let's be clear: Most books are meant to be engaged with, to be enjoyed, and if your shelves are cluttered, you defeat that purpose. Most titles are not the elite ones mentioned above. Your book keeping needs to make sense to your personal collection. The ones you love and treasure may be under lock and key like mine or you may only keep classics for ready reference. Whichever genre your personality falls into, finding your titles with ease among the stacks is the guiding principle. Personalize your library like your reading list so that your titles are there for you when you need them — just like old friends.

THE WAY
Keep your bookshelves up to date with books that you love and want to read — for the first time or over and over again.

DAILY PRACTICES

✓ Organize your bookshelves, and pare down when you can. If you have books in boxes and storage, you defeat the reason for having them to begin with. This week plan a thoughtful purge, and release your literary gems from storage.

✓ Make a reading plan and a reading list. Once you have cleared out what you won't read, you can create a fantastic reading list that is just waiting to be discovered.

✓ Bookshelves fill up quickly and can be easily cluttered, so it is important to maintain them. Have a one-in-one-out philosophy if that works for you, or plan a monthly updating. When you can't see the spines of your books, you are keeping too many.

✓ Use the rule of less is more, and put same-sized books together. Hardcovers make better display items than paperbacks, so group those together. If you need to keep paperbacks, shelve them behind a more attractive hardcover stack.

✓ Keeping a "must read" pile can help you organize and find what you want to read next. Do not buy anything new until you finish your reading pile.

✓ Take the pressure off when reading for pleasure. Stop reading if you are having trouble "getting into" a book. Being in the mood to read something is a relevant emotion when reading, so honor the mood you're in, and find a title to match it.

The Beauty of Unitasking

JOB OPENING: COMPETENT *multitasking banking professional able to juggle and manage a variety of different projects under tremendous time constraints and deliver top-notch results.* My neighbor — a competent banking professional — answered this ad when looking for a new job. I wondered how he or anyone, for that matter, could possibly deliver top-notch results when being asked to juggle multiple projects at one time. My philosophy is that humans can do only one thing at a time to do it well.

Unlike computers that jump effortlessly from one screen to another, never forgetting where they left off or being interrupted from their tasks at hand, humans do not task jump with the same results. We get distracted by our mothers calling on line two, the instant-messaging alert blinking on the screen, or the coworker who's always chatting in the next cubicle. Even the television screen is multitasking with that crawl at the bottom that tells you additional headline news while you are watching the headline news. Or the promo box on the corner of the screen that alerts you to the next time the show you are currently watching will be on again. These innovations reinforce the fact that we need to do multiple things at a time to keep pace. More importantly, it makes us think that we can get everything done simultaneously and makes that the priority.

If you think about the job listing for the banker, you will realize the flaw in the listing. In this age of more is more, it seems the hiring manager is trying to squeeze every drop out of this one employee regardless of whether the workload expectation is realistic. But the question becomes whether all this multitasking makes us better workers or makes it only *seem* like we are doing more. According to many recent studies, multitasking is taking not only a toll on our productivity but also on our ability to focus. As we jump from project to project or task to task, we actually lose valuable time. Constant switching causes us to repeatedly gear up for each activity — in essence, to reboot each task as we jump back and forth. Losing continuity results in duplicating efforts and actually wasting, not saving, time.

According to neuroscientist Earl Miller, "People can't multitask very well, and when people say they can, they're deluding themselves; we simply can't focus on more than one thing at a time." He explains that we are not doing two things at one time — such as the banking job required — but rather we are switching very rapidly between two tasks. A good client of mine advocates "unitasking," or concentrating on doing one thing at a time before starting something new. When he multitasks, he often makes mistakes that he has to correct later. I would ask the hiring manager which would be preferable, several half-started projects or two projects brought to completion with detail and precision. It is time to laud unitasking and the excellent results it provides.

THE WAY
Understand that multitasking is an impossible notion unless you're doing mindless, repetitious chores. What you are really doing is "task jumping," or switching from task to task rapidly. Adopting a slower pace, where concentration and focus are needed, will help you complete projects.

DAILY PRACTICES

✓ Recognize the occurrence of multitasking in your daily routine and how it affects your mental state and productivity. Begin by determining which multitasking activities can be harmful, such as talking on a cell phone while driving or helping your child do homework while watching television.

✓ Enjoy healthy multitasking like folding laundry while watching a movie or shredding papers while listening to music, all of which involve two passive activities that don't require as much as focus as one active task. Recognize the difference between this level of tasks and those that you have deemed dangerous to practice together.

✓ To help keep on track "time block" your day: Determine your big projects, and schedule time to work on them without interruption. Let the other less-necessary tasks take second place in your day.

✓ When interrupted, make a conscious effort to note where you left off. This will help you get back to speed faster with the task you left behind.

✓ Are you addicted to TV? Is it the first thing you turn on in the morning, the last thing you turn off at night? Television often provides a distracting backdrop to everything we do. Notice the focus gained by monitoring your usage.

✓ Make a conscious effort to become a better listener. Stay focused on the person you are talking with, not the one vying for your attention.

42

Practice Forgiveness

I HAD A guy friend whom I shared everything with. We were drinking buddies, soul mates, confidants, and each other's best friends. Remaining single through most of our thirties, we had much to commiserate about and usually did so over carefree cocktails at our local hangout. We never worried about when we would get married or, in fact, if we even would get married. We were having a good time being single. When Kevin met his future wife, Cynthia, our fun times came to an abrupt end. There was now a third, more important, party in the picture who did not want to play second fiddle to a drinking buddy from the past. She needed to come first and rightfully so. Slowly but surely I was fazed out of Kevin's life — a painful adjustment for me.

Life has a habit of sending you the same lesson over and over again until you master it. Five years later when my husband and I were dating, the same thing happened with his best gal pal, Susan. As had happened to me, Susan was being shut out and forced to realign her friendship boundaries. Life had sent me the same exact situation only in reverse, and I was able to slip my feet firmly into another person's shoes.

This awkward dance continued through the first three years of our marriage, where each of us would smile cordially with nothing behind the smile. And then something changed. Susan had an epiphany. (Perhaps she realized that I was not going anywhere.) She asked me to forgive her actions. Having been on the receiving end of the relationship with Cynthia and Kevin, I was moved by Susan's bold gesture and honesty.

What could I do but forgive? I think I surprised myself when I said, "I have been exactly where you are, and I know how it feels." More than anything else, I wanted to move on — move on from both awkward relationships. And so we did. With that weight lifted off my shoulder, I felt clear.

About a month later, Kevin sent me an e-mail. He, too, was ready to move on. (See WAY #5: there are no coincidences — as this noncoincidence of timing proves.) We met for a drink just like old times, and it was apparent that we were both ready to forgive as well as forget. That's the thing about forgiveness: once you let go of that anger, you are opened up to a larger capacity of emotion. I created space for good things by letting go of the bad.

THE WAY
Holding on to the negativity of the past can often prevent us from experiencing positive emotions like compassion, forgiveness, and love. When you harbor resentment and regret in your thoughts, they breed more of the same.

DAILY PRACTICES

✓ Is a negative relationship from the past preventing you from moving on to the future? If you have not practiced the art of forgiveness, incorporate it into your lifestyle now. Using the rule of "How will I feel about this in five years?" as a guideline, remember the value of the relationship, not the animosity of the breakup.

✓ Love means being able to say you are sorry. Don't mistake hurt feelings for anger and act out with vengeance.

Recognizing the difference between anger and hurt can help you get on the road to forgiveness with little regret. Be brave enough to voice your hurt.

✓ Sometimes forgiveness seems like the least likely thing you can do, but when you do it, you realize that it opens up space in your heart for more positive emotions. Embrace the idea of rising above the situation. You will become more able to handle negativity with grace.

✓ People make mistakes — it is a part of our human make-up. To forgive shows your capacity to adapt and move on. Think of how many times you wish to be forgiven for something, and use that as a guideline for forgiving others.

✓ Are you able to forgive yourself? We often spend time beating ourselves up about things from our past, which we cannot change or control. Self-forgiveness is as important as forgiving another. Write yourself an apology note for things you have not been able to let go of, and mail it to yourself.

✓ Spiritual leaders such as the Dalai Lama, Jesus, and Krishna teach that the power of forgiveness will result in a new level of awareness. Work on your empathy and your compassion. If you can forgive your enemies, eventually you will become a more evolved and enlightened person. Looking through the lens of people doing their best at all times enables you to forgive and, more importantly, to forget.

I AM SCHEDULED to do a wardrobe makeover for Carol, a new client who lives in Manhattan. When we book her session, I am confused; the address she gives me is in New Jersey. Apparently, she has been housing 20 years of clothing at her parents' house nearly 40 minutes away from her place. And when I say

43

Crowded House

"clothing," I mean every piece of clothing she has ever worn. She has bins and racks and closets full of every outfit from every stage of her life. The time is ticking on this makeover because her parents are downsizing and moving to Florida and have refused to take her clothing with them. The clutterer ultimatum has been issued when mother tells daughter, "If you don't come here and deal with this mess, it is all going to the Salvation Army."

Carol panics; she has no choice but to show up to sort out the details of her cluttered wardrobe so that she can save her favorites. And like so many clutterers before her, she has attempted this weeding out on several occasions before. But the task was so daunting that she gave up. I explain the "third-session setback." In organizing terms this is the period that comes after a few successful sessions, when the work gets harder and the decisions more complicated. This usually happens around the third or fourth session, causing many to give up. (In my fantasy movie version, this would be the scene where the music crescendos, and our heroine rises from the closet floor and begins to sort and purge with a one-two punch.)

Clutter can be a hard-fought battle — scary and daunting and seemingly impossible without help. Many think that

more time is the remedy, but Carol's clutter unfortunately was not going to be eliminated just one bin at a time and certainly not in the allotted time frame. Last count of the bins and racks was over 50! That amounts to about 45 more weekends than she has. It's time to call in the cavalry, and that is me and her best friend, Dan, who is someone she trusts and is familiar with her malady. This is a bonus: I never think three is a crowd — I see more hands to lift and tote.

When she calls me to talk over her problem, she is still focusing backward and explains her closest attempt to purge was when her mother donated 12 items to the Salvation Army thrift store. When Carol returned home and saw which 12 items they were, she immediately panicked, ran to the store, and purchased the items back — plus she made a generous donation to the store for their trouble. Of course it was no trouble at all for the volunteer worker who happily took the money and made the sale. But for Carol any 12 items might have triggered that meltdown. Dan and I will need to get to the root of why this unused, neglected clothing holds so much emotion for Carol.

"Tell me about what is there — the Levis you wore during your first kiss, a wedding gown, a high school recital dress?" No, no, and no, she says. "It's more like clothing from first dates that went nowhere, suits from three jobs ago, and costumes from an abandoned acting career." Carol's closet clutter comes with a puzzling twist: Her clothing often holds a *bad* memory. She is keeping a time capsule of every unpleasant experience she ever had simply because it was part of her past. In Carol's case it is more than nostalgia and more than the "I can wear that again" syndrome. It is as if she may somehow be able to rewrite the past, replacing the bad with good — and should that fantasy ever arrive, she will be fully costumed.

But this kind of rewind only happens in science fiction. The key to Carol and her Peter Pan syndrome has more to do with forgiveness for past mistakes. Regret is what holds her to these outfits. She regrets decisions she made, relationships that did not work out, and careers that did not flourish. To let go of the clothing would make her come to terms with the past. Now the past has caught up with her, and she is being forced to deal with it — and quickly. The universe has swept in, sweeping her parents off to Florida, sweeping away her childhood home, and sweeping away all those outfits from the '80s.

Carol's clutter problem has become a family problem, and as a good daughter, Carol's lightbulb finally clicks on. When clutter begins to get in the way of relationships, it is time to let go; it is time to say good-bye. This shift is what she needed to take responsibility for her things, to grow up and finally leave the nest. With the help of her mom, Dan, and a few Salvation Army pickups, the house has been cleared. Carol takes with her one bin of nostalgic clothing that holds good memories — and the rest, as they say, is history.

THE WAY
Avoid romanticizing and emotionalizing the past so much that anything that links to it seems irreplaceable.

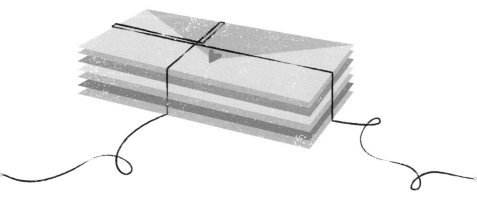

DAILY PRACTICES

✓ What is holding you back? Time, space, motivation, or energy? Examine the reasons that cause you to shift your items instead of sorting your items. Moving them to an out-of-sight location is one way to remove the task from being pressing, so examine where as well as why you keep your nostalgic pieces.

✓ Fashion trends do return but are always tweaked enough to look modern. Review your nostalgic pieces and note if they are ready for the time capsule or ready to wear. Use the rule of taking part in a trend only the first time around to keep you age and fashion appropriate.

✓ Clothing can remind us of the past, but it doesn't hold the only memory for what we have done and who we are. So let that coat go and realize that your memories are in your heart and mind, not in the clothing you wore. If an article of clothing recalls a bad memory, all the more reason to let it go!

✓ Not knowing where to donate useful items is a strong excuse for keeping virtually anything. Recognize when this makes you hold on instead of letting you move on. With the abundance of charities and local shelters, you are one Google search away from releasing the items to someone in need.

✓ We often consider our clothing to be financial investments that continue to pay dividends over time. Just because something was expensive does not mean that it holds its value like a good stock or that you should keep it.

✓ There are valid reasons for keeping some old pieces in your wardrobe. But when there is a preponderance of go-go boots or fraternity sweatshirts, use your editing skills to store only a few in a memory box that you tuck away for future generations.

THE WORD "SHOULD" is a part of life. On any given day, we use the word dozens of times: We should watch what we eat, we should read more, we should exercise more often. . . . Many of us *should* our way through life, from jobs we should keep, to friends that we should keep in touch with, and habits we should practice, simply because we always have. When you think about how many times you use the word,

44

Eliminate "Should" from Your Vocabulary

notice how much time is spent thinking negatively about what you think you *should* be doing versus what you actually *are* doing. We feel as if we are being kept from what we would like to be doing, and it becomes a self-fulfilling prophecy that robs us of our enjoyment of life.

"Should" goes hand in hand with how we challenge ourselves and can propel us to do better, but it also can make us feel as if we are never doing enough. We can balance the yin and yang of the word by accepting that we are exactly where we need to be. This age-old philosophy can often be difficult to put into practice — particularly in the modern world where tempting choices abound.

For example, my local yoga studio offered a value pack of classes at a discount price. If you had planned to attend more than 12 classes in three months, the value would be hard to beat. Given that logic, I bought the pack, even though I knew it would be a challenge to make all 12 classes in the allotted time frame. I also knew intuitively that my usual pay-per-class status was the better choice for me. My decision to purchase was based on what I thought I should be doing, not what I would actually do. In the end, I didn't use the value pack, and in the future I plan to follow my instinct of how I live and practice yoga: one class at a time.

These snap decisions cause us to litter our datebooks, cloud our minds, and make us do things out of pressure instead of taking the time to consider our motivations. Granted, we all have obligations, but when there are too many of them in your daily life, a review is needed. The number of activities that you love should be equal to if not more than your obligations.

Serial-planner Dennis is a victim of calendar "should"s. Each Monday morning he looks at his datebook and wonders why he has made so many plans. Most of his Monday morning is then spent rescheduling. He describes it as somebody else inhabiting his body when he schedules four nights in a row of martini drinking. At the moment he makes the plan, he disconnects from his desires and gives in to obligation. Making the plan in advance makes it seem more feasible somehow, as if he will be able to achieve that kind of pace come the actual date. But he is only delaying the inevitable phone call to cancel. If his ability matched his desire from the get-go, he would arrive at the right number of evenings

out — be it three, one, or even none. Imagine the time and anxiety he would save every Monday.

Dennis, like others, is ready for a thoughtful review of the role of "should" in his life. I ask him — and challenge you — to find out this week: Are your activities enjoyable? Do they achieve your goals at work, or are they something born out of obligation and take time? Taking a few steps to stop and reflect before penning in a commitment can create a life you look forward to, not one you should be looking forward to.

THE WAY
If you are engaging too much of your time in what you *should* be doing, you are missing out on what you *love* to do. Adjust your thinking, and increase your happiness.

DAILY PRACTICES

✓ If your plans for the week fill you with a sense of dread, it is time to make a change. Ideally, your plans should bring you happiness, not a faulty sense of obligation. Making your obligations in harmony with your heart's desire is this week's task.

✓ We all have commitments and obligations that are less pleasant than others, but if we constantly put ourselves into situations that are not fulfilling, we will merely be going through the motions without truly enjoying our lives. Constantly imagining ourselves in a future better situation leads us to wishing our life away.

✓ "Should" often goes hand in hand with guilt, where we want to be doing something else. When you examine the things that you should be doing, be careful to note if you are avoiding commitment or simply putting unrealistic expectations on your plate. "Should" makes us uncomfortable with the choices we made. Instead, make your expectations more realistic, and you will feel more comfortable with your choices.

✓ Downtime and entertainment are as necessary to our growth as obligations and commitments — but be careful not to misinterpret your disinterest in doing something that is necessary. Blowing things off because you deem them unpleasant is the other end of the spectrum. Balance the necessary with thoughtful play and leisure time.

✓ "Should" does not put you in the driver's seat; it forces you to imagine something else while you are engaging in a chosen activity. Instead of escaping from the present moment to fantasize about a more perfect activity you could be engaged in, realize that you make your own choices to be exactly where you are.

✓ Release the grip that "should" has on your daily activity. Guilt and insecurity often go hand in hand with this kind of behavior, especially when we use it to review past mistakes. Eliminate the word entirely, and replace it with the phrase, "In the future, the best thing I can do is . . ."

REAL-ESTATE GURU SANDY

Turbulence

was a top performer in a premier Los Angeles firm. Her ability to respond to clients' needs at a moment's notice made her indispensable to her company, and she often saw clients on nights and weekends. "If you want something done, give it to a busy person" is a cliché that seems to have been written about her, as if she were in a race to get as much done as fast as she can regardless of the importance. This frenzied lifestyle did not go unnoticed by one of her clients, a top yoga master. When he invited her to a class, she opted to try it, thinking that it would be a great way to meet new clients. Plus the challenging yoga poses became another task to master and then cross off her list.

Unaware of the spiritual aspects that the controlled breathing and mindfulness of the practice were doing for her soul, she went to yoga simply to exercise and network. The immediate results were, indeed, a toned body and a larger Rolodex. But other lessons were working on a subconscious level and emerged just when she needed them most during a harrowing cross-country flight. When the plane hit violent weather, she began to panic. Alone and scared, she recalled the lessons of yoga and began the breathing exercises she had learned. This helped her remain calm in the face of a terrifying situation. And suddenly the meaning of yoga struck her like a lightning bolt, which was, oddly enough, what was striking her plane at that moment. She finally grasped why the yoga master told her to pace herself.

The plane landed safely, and Sandy was forever changed. Today she practices yoga every chance she gets and has left

the world of real estate to pursue a teaching career, which gives her time to devote to her two sons. She prides herself on her ability to turn off work and focus solely on her children's needs, whether they are discussing skateboarding or sharing a family meal. And while she still has a to-do list, she checks things off methodically and thoughtfully and operates from this tenet: Tomorrow is just another opportunity to let things flow.

> **THE WAY**
> Life is not graded on how fast you can move through it but rather how much you can enjoy it.

DAILY PRACTICES

✓ If your to-do list has become an overburdening, unachievable goal, simply release it into the universe. Try a day without list making, and see what living in the experience of now provides for you.

✓ Are you moving at breakneck speed from one task to another not knowing what to do next? If you finish the day with a feeling of amnesia, such as "I can't even recall what happened today," it is time to slow down and limit your tasks.

✓ A good indicator of doing too much is repeatedly having to revisit the same task to make it right. Resist the urge to do things faster, which can often cause mistakes. You actually save time by doing things right the first time with a slower and more methodical approach.

✓ Find a way to make your to-do list work for you. Centralize your numerous notes, thoughts, and phone numbers in one notebook. Creating one consistent place saves you time hunting down multiple Post-its and notes.

✓ Technology encourages us to respond as quickly as possible. Trying to match technology's speed can cause hasty, often injudicious, decision making. Always consider your words before hitting the send button.

✓ Schedules lacking any free time or leeway force playing catch-up when an unexpected problem arises. To deal with unforeseen obstacles and keep them from derailing your entire day, practice a "Murphy's Law" approach by setting up time buffers in your schedule.

46

Mexican Soup

CLAIRE HAS BEEN working on a book proposal for two years. She wants it to be perfect before she sends it out to any publisher. In an effort to refine the book idea, she has been seeking feedback from fellow writers, editors, and just about anyone willing to read and comment. Additionally, she joined a writer's group and has taken two classes on proposal writing, which resulted in reams of notes. When we meet in a seminar I am doing on how to get organized, Claire tells me she is looking for someone to help organize her notes.

I hear this problem from writers often; they crave a road map from those who traveled this path before them. Many think that *my* path should be *their* path, and that is simply not the case. (Unless you are a shopaholic turned organizer who likes to share her experiences, in which case I have tailor-made advice!) In reality, the writing process, like organizing, is not one size fits all. When I help Claire, I discover that it is not her notes that need organizing. In fact, she has become so proficient at organizing — her notes, her files, and everything else externally related to the writing process are color coded and in chronological order — that her last organizing foray resulted in a streamlined, freshly painted office. No, organizing is not her issue; too much external input is.

> Unlocking the door to your creativity may lie in honoring your voice first — because the truth speaks volumes.

Her story brings to mind a book I read as a child called *Mexican Soup*. In the story, the mother of a large family is preparing dinner. As she begins to shop for the ingredients to make a soup that will please everybody, she has a discussion with each family member — and each person has a different ingredient to leave out of the soup. Her husband does not like mushrooms, her son hates tomatoes, her daughter thinks spinach is gross, and her mother cannot eat potatoes. By the time she has consulted with everyone in the family, the mother is left with no ingredients. Later, as she spoons out the soup, she tells her family that each of their requests has

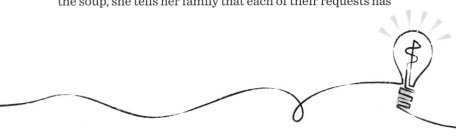

been honored. Based on their preferences, the end result is a bowl of hot water with no ingredients at all.

When you ask for everyone's opinion, you sometimes dilute the overall impact and end up in a quandary about how to proceed — be it a tasty soup or a book proposal. I tell Claire to be selective about the advice she takes. After a long discussion about her book, we come up with an overarching theme for her memoir, a love story that rings true to her. Unlocking the door to your creativity may lie in honoring your voice first — because the truth speaks volumes.

THE WAY
When it comes to creativity, to your own self be true.

DAILY PRACTICES

✓ Feedback can be a powerful tool to self-improvement, but too much of it can be confusing and misleading. It is important to know your audience; a few like-minded advisers instead of a wide-ranging group may not represent your ideal reader.

✓ Pleasing others if taken too far can leave you feeling unsatisfied. Rule one is to first make sure you are happy with your work, and then ask others for feedback. Be mindful that you can always take or leave the comments offered.

✓ When beginning any creative process, think big. Corral your ideas and creativity in one place. Editing and honing your art is the second stage; the first is idea generation, which begins with giving your inner editor the day off.

✓ The idea of perfection is something that all artists struggle with. At a certain point in the creative process, it is important to let go and let your message be shared. Nothing will ever be 100 percent perfect, so work on getting the project to a level that you are proud of, not one that embodies an unattainable goal.

✓ If you are laboring over the same project for years and getting nowhere, try pitching your message in one or two descriptive sentences. If you are having a problem with this part of the process, you may need to be clearer about what your project is.

✓ Creativity is often a mix of struggle and joy, but if a project is sapping the life out of you, you may be simply pursuing the wrong project. Refine your idea to create your version of the perfect soup this week. Chances are if you like what you have created, someone else will, too.

There Is No Me in Wii

MY HUSBAND TELLS me that "we" need to lose weight. This use of the word "we" never means anything other than "you." I know this because we have been married for five years, and I have learned a few things — like how to compromise, consider positive word choices, and, most of all, choose my battles. And this is exactly what I am doing

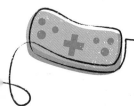

when for Christmas this year, instead of individual gifts, "we" opted to buy "Wii Fitness."

Frank is thrilled about the great deal he got online and even more thrilled that our recent homebody status as new parents will lend itself to something positive — like working off the holiday cookies that we seem to eat in double digits in one sitting. I am dubious about this purchase even though we will be able to play softball, golf, and run an obstacle course in the comfort of our living room. Cementing my status as a good team player, I give him a high five.

We get busy creating a "Mii," which seems in opposition to our new team philosophy. My Mii, or avatar, personality is a curly-headed sprite wearing rose-colored glasses. I call her — well, me — "Hot Stuff." Frank opts for a tall, angular looking Mii, which he names "The Dude." We are already keeping score, which calls to mind some advice my mother dispensed when I was newly married. Keeping score in a marriage never works, she cautioned. But Wii is asking us to do exactly that: log our activity minutes and calories burned in a constant tally of who is winning. In fact, the leading Mii is often given a little crown to wear, showing the others who is the winner.

The first few nights Frank commandeers the controls. By the time he is ready to hand it over, I am too tired to start, so I feel a bit like a Wii widow. I retire to bed to do a crossword puzzle, a game that does not judge me — at least publicly. The next night I change my attitude to a winning one where I conquer the Wii, not vice versa. But when I check my age through one of the confusing concentration and balance tests, the Wii tells me that my actual age is 61. I am shamed. Committed to not let the Wii win, I summon the *Rocky* theme music and every other sports mantra I can think of. I

finally settle on the phrase "it is not the size of the dog in the fight but the size of the fight in the dog."

Each day I engage in the battle, I push through the discomfort. The going gets tough, and I get going. I don't tell my husband what I am up to, but he sees my usage. We have no secrets. It comes up on my status calendar, even though I locked my profile. And the next time I test my weight and real age, I have lost three pounds, and I am 34. Frank has lost one pound and is stuck at 58 — but who is keeping score? Although we may want to avoid it initially, discomfort is a necessary process to our growth. Discomfort is there for a reason, offering a glimpse at the other side, a reward to a journey of hard work. As for Frank and me, we are making it work.

THE WAY
Working through the sticky situations in your life is part of the growth process. Look at them as a key element in reaching your goal.

DAILY PRACTICES

✓ Competition can be a healthy motivator to make change, but some competition clouds our judgment. Make the competition with yourself rather than with others — or others' standards. Only you can measure true success.

✓ Recognize the unique position you are in right now, and embrace it. Use that as a starting point to where you want to be, and let go of the way you used to be, what you used to weigh, or how good your hair used to look. Looking back nostalgically at our youth can often block the wisdom that comes with aging gracefully.

✓ Take your embarrassment IQ. Are you always worried about how you will look to others? Eliminate the outside influences that cause you to follow someone else's path. If your journey includes a cheering section, you may be missing the point of self-fulfillment.

✓ Give your goals a reality check this week, and set a plan for slow, steady progress toward achievable expectations. Think thoughtfully about goals and an appropriate time frame for meeting them. Know that disappointments are often a result of a goal set too high, too soon.

✓ Define your discomfort level by adopting an easy attitude when a sticky situation arises. Training ourselves to dealing with life's not-so-happy moments prepares us to handle difficulty. A change in attitude can create calmness, where solution finding is easier.

Lose the Cape

EMILY IS LIVING her life in duplicate; she is straddling two jobs, two children, and two aging parents who, ironically, live two doors down. She hit rock bottom when she spent an entire evening searching her car for her Life scribe pen, which stored everything she needed for a client presentation the following day. This special pen not only served as a writing instrument. it was also a recorder of the client's notes. She needed this pen and could not afford to lose it — and the time it took to find it was setting her even further behind.

Emily is a longtime college friend who felt compelled to e-mail me after this incident. She wanted me to talk her out of her mental clutter. This was a surprising e-mail to get from Emily, who excelled at everything she did. In college, she chaired fundraisers and was the president of her sorority, all while maintaining a 4.0 grade-point average. Clearly there was much more here than simply misplacing a pen, albeit a special multipurpose one. I immediately gave her a call.

As is the case with so many clients I deal with, once I heard her story, the answers seemed fairly obvious. She had begun to explain that working full time and starting a new business was putting stress on her relationships and family when I stopped her with a question. "It is hard enough to balance one job with family commitments, so how can you do *two* jobs full time and do them both well?" I asked. She told me that her successful corporate career was reaching its end, but she was having trouble letting go. Even though she had made all the financial plans to ensure a successful

start-up and had clients lined up to work with her, something was still holding her back.

With a little coaxing, she admitted that she thought she should be able to handle it all — the two jobs, the two kids, the two parents — like a modern day Noah. "I want an extraordinary life!" she exclaimed. I sighed, then said simply, "Lose the cape." Emily giggled her trademark giggle (she laughs more easily than most) and waited to hear what I had to say. "Your life is already extraordinary," I told her, "but let's leave that aside for a minute. Right now let's get you in a place where you can find your pen." And she laughed even harder.

Sometimes it takes something mundane (like misplacing a pen) to ground you, get you back to reality. This is common for people who simply do too much. And that is what happened to extraordinary Emily and her extraordinary life. In trying to do it all, she managed to be everywhere and nowhere at the same time. Meanwhile, as she planned for her future, her present was escaping her. We decided that two full-time jobs are obviously too much for any one person to manage. And with the help of her financial adviser and the good fortune of having clients who would last her through the first year of her business, Emily took the leap into entrepreneurship and left her corporate life. The result is a schedule of her own making where she calls the shots on her still extraordinary life.

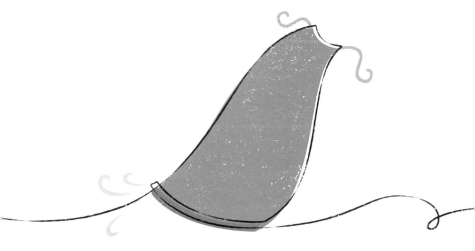

> **THE WAY**
> If something new is going to enter into your life, you need to make room for it.

DAILY PRACTICES

✓ Lose the cape. Be mindful of doing too much, which can often cause you to set unrealistic goals.

✓ When you spend your time thinking of "someday," you often neglect the steps you need to get there. Take the time to pause on the necessary moments that contribute to the end result.

✓ Realizing your true priorities is the first step to achieving them. If your current lifestyle and habits take you away from living a more fulfilling life, it is time to have a life review of your priorities. Start with a simple list of what is important to you.

✓ Be resourceful when thinking about a career change. Take the time to research and read about other career paths. You might look into taking a class or consulting a local business organization to learn more. Working for yourself is a difficult undertaking but can be fulfilling if you crave more freedom and flexibility.

✓ Create a professional asset list with the skills you have learned throughout your career. How will these skills adapt to a new profession? For example, could an affinity to arbitrate disputes between coworkers mean you have

a calling for law or mediation? You may have more of a path than you realize.

✓ Get more information about a new direction. Ask people you know who are living your dream for advice. Most entrepreneurs are willing to talk about their experience. But first research what questions to ask so that you can respect their time as well as their generosity.

49

A Fashionista in Paris

I DECIDE TO fly to Paris with my good friend Jane, the world's best shopper. This could be very bad for my American Express bill but very good for my fashion sense. I rationalize the money I saved using frequent-flyer miles for the flight and the free hotel that Jane has offered and immediately see dollar signs. For some reason vacations always seem to offer a kind of buy-it-no-matter-what attitude. And this trip is no different because I am shopping with the super shopper of the century, a woman known in our intimate circle as "Shoppie."

Before her seasonal closet cleaning sessions, an e-mail goes out to select people who have the same shoe size and sense of style. Friends show up on a first-come, first-served basis to go through Jane's castoffs. This is how I scored my Cynthia Rowley shoes and my first and only Marc Jacobs bag. (Who cares that it was from two seasons ago?) When the opportunity comes up to shop in Paris with a pro, I am in. This is valuable firsthand experience. I have been here before, encouraged to buy clothes suited for someone else, even though I have yet to wear the Chanel suit from my last trip. At home, I dress like a teenage boy with layers of short-sleeve T-shirts worn over long sleeve T-shirts. On vacation, another person emerges: a scarf-donning woman of ulti-mate sophistication.

I had so much to learn! The first day I am intimidated by Jane's knowledge of the Prada pointy-toe flat. She knows all the floral and plaid patterns by season and has an encyclo-pedic knowledge of which stores have her size and which styles she cannot purchase in New York. This also goes for Annick Goutal perfume; although they do sell it in Saks Fifth Avenue, it is not the same strength as the variety bought in the flagship Saint Germain store, nor are the same scents available. I observe Jane in her natural habitat, the Hermes store where she purchases a few bangles in this season's patterns.

Day two is for flea markets, where vintage Chanel broaches and mint-condition wrap coats are just waiting to be scooped up. I buy a never-worn vintage French-blue coat with a raccoon collar for $90. It is not designer, but I love it just the same because it takes advan-tage of something very French: the second-hand store. I marvel at the quality of the merchandise, which appears brand new. Jane whispers that many of the Hermes scarves are last season's patterns. But it is with her knowledge of all things designer that I combine her addiction to the wisdom of the French. Solange, our salesperson, tells me that in France ladies choose one or two signature items per season and then the next year get something new. I have found my niche. And with that, Solange and Shoppie encourage me to buy a Hermes scarf, slightly used, in a classic equestrian pattern. As a suburban mall girl who never got on a horse until later in life, the theme is a bit of a stretch, but they tell me I have to have it.

By the week's end my purchases are few: the coat, the scarf, a bottle of Annick Goutal perfume, and a few pairs of chandelier earrings. On the other side of the hotel room, Jane has lined up bags and bags of the holy trinity: Chanel, Hermes, and Prada. Having purchased my heart's desires, I no longer feel intimidated by her bounty.

When I try on the scarf at home, it is hard to manage. I try to make it a belt, a top, a wrap, or an ascot. I wear it with my new coat, but it just never sits right. I keep it for a few months or so, and then one day I find it at the back of my accessory drawer. I realize that the scarf is just not my style, and I am prepared to let it go — and like a good French fashionista, I sell it on eBay. The student has become the master.

THE WAY
Personal style is something only you can define, so make fashion choices that are right for you.

DAILY PRACTICES

✓ Consignment stores and eBay are great ways to relieve buyer's remorse and recoup a little cash. Let wasted money be a cautionary tale to buy thoughtfully, not impulsively.

✓ Put together your real-life uniform — the best pieces embody your style, fit, and comfort. Note the attributes of those favorite pieces, and guarantee use by letting those criteria guide future purchases.

✓ Exercise caution when buying in multiples. When you buy something in every color, will most be given away at season's end? Consider making one smart purchase over several.

✓ Just because something is trendy does not mean that you have to take part in the trend. Most runway fashion is difficult to incorporate into a working wardrobe. Accessorize with a smaller piece, such as a scarf or belt, rather than buying into the entire trend.

✓ Be age conscious by resisting the temptation to dive into your daughter's closet even though you can fit into most of her jeans. Dressing age appropriately helps you to look confident.

✓ We often convince ourselves that vacations are once-in-a-lifetime opportunities to spend. Going on vacation does not mean you should buy everything you see. Avoid big bills by choosing a few select items to buy before setting down on the Champs-Élysées.

The Big Break

IT CAN BE hard for people to pinpoint the most-defining moments of their lives. The word "moment" itself is used for a variety of situations these days, from seeking the ordinary and meaningful moments in everyday life to experiencing that moment on stage when a performer truly connects with an audience. When I think about a moment, I think of its fleeting nature and how it can instantly transcend an experience and leave the participants forever changed. For this reason my favorite television show is *American Idol*; the judges are constantly looking for the contestants to have "a moment," and for the contestants it equates to a chance of a lifetime or their "big break."

But big breaks can come in different forms for different people, as is illustrated by Steve, an energetic physical trainer with a large slate of clients, a growing family, and a music career on the side. He researches the latest alternative medicine for his clients, he experiments with Pilates and Tai Chi, and he jams on the weekend with his band. Steve is in constant motion and struggles to fit it all in. But his big break was not a musical one. On a Saturday afternoon, when rushing from the gym to a gig, he was hoisting his drum kit and gym bag into his van when he heard a snap. At first he thought it was his equipment, but a sharp pain in his wrist immediately indicated otherwise. His gig was canceled, his list of clients diminished, and his extracurricular classes were put on hold. Steve's healing period had begun. He was forced to slow down.

Living slowly and mindfully is taking hold all over the world, whether you have been recently downsized, forced

onto the sidelines with an injury, or had a relationship end. The lesson of stopping and appreciating is inherent in all that we do, and for the American way, where faster has always been better, this lesson provides the converse ideology. Steve's literal big break soon provided many moments of appreciation. Taking his children to school and to the park became possible without the intrusion of jam sessions and classes. Jumping into the kitchen to make his signature pizza for dinner was doable again. And reconnecting with his wife, listening to music, was rediscovered as a way to unwind from the day. He tells me his life has been forever changed, that he was doing too much and breaking his wrist was the best thing that ever happened to him.

To me, a physical person who loves to exercise, being sidelined for any reason looks like the worst possible thing to have happen — but life is funny that way. Sometimes you experience a moment when not only did you not plan on it but it doesn't look anything like you thought it would.

> **THE WAY**
> Big breaks can come to us when we least expect them and reveal unforeseen gifts.

DAILY PRACTICES

✓ Setbacks can shine a light on a good outcome to follow. Our emotions often make us think that things are much worse than they seem, yet if we view things as temporary, we can often adopt a "this too shall pass" mentality.

✓ What is your approach for dealing with adversity? Do you adopt absolute language like "everything" and "always"? Avoid unmovable thinking, and adopt a more carefree attitude. Making absolute statements limits our ability to move through adversity with grace.

✓ Appreciate your ability to bounce back by noting how you dealt with adverse situations in the past. Trust in your innate ability to weather the next storm as you have done in the past. You will be well prepared to find a silver lining.

✓ Perspective is necessary when an unexpected event derails your everyday life. It is difficult to perceive the high of a good experience without the contrasting perspective of a bad one. Both are necessary forces for balance, and one cannot exist without the other.

✓ Analyze your tolerance level when a bad situation happens. Are you able to resolve the problem without overreacting? How we choose to view a situation and present it to others can change our thoughts and feelings, so be your own public relations manager, and keep matters in perspective.

✓ The best way to let things get you down is to dwell on them at length. The past is not something you can change, so belaboring what you might have said or done is counterproductive. Take responsibility for your actions, behave with good intentions, and, above all, keep moving forward.

51

Teach Your Children Well

SARAH IS A recent magna cum laude graduate of Yale who has just landed her dream job as an assistant trader. She appears to have it all: great education, great new job, even a great new wardrobe. I was referred to Sarah through another organizer who decided that Sarah's organizing job was too big for her.

Never one to back off from a challenge, I accept, certain that I have seen the same hoarding scenarios in countless other clients. But this time, there is a twist; the job needs to be completed before the delivery of Sarah's first baby. A new mother myself, I know the joyful disarray that babies bring and realize that this may be Sarah's last chance to get organized for quite some time. Thrilled by the challenge, I am hopeful that the pressure and my personal experience may make Sarah move quickly.

I enter the home she shares with her mother (her recently deceased grandmother lived there, as well) and find that there is little room to get inside. The entire living area is so packed with clutter that the furniture isn't even visible. Making matters worse, the windows are shrouded with dark curtains, shutting out any light source. And all I can think of is the baby. *I have to help the baby!* A new generation is about

to be born, and I don't want the little one to be a hoarder. Hoarding is a hereditary problem; how you teach your children to deal with their possessions can be passed down. It is clear from this client and her family that some recognition of their problem is apparent, but whether the ladies can create enough space for the new generation is the question. They will need to let go of lifelong patterns for the benefit of the child. And this can be easier said than done.

I immediately want to see where the baby will live. Sarah points over stacks of Rubbermaid bins that line the hallway to the room recently vacated by her grandmother, who clearly also had the hoarding disease. Both Sarah and her mother have had a hard time clearing out this room because they want to be respectful to the grandmother's memory. I explain that creating a clean space for the baby takes priority; the time has come to let go of past habits for the right reason. At the moment, however, baby gifts, baby furniture, baby clothing, and parenting books all lie atop Grandma's possessions, which are all still in place. I feel a bit overwhelmed myself.

Leaving the future nursery for now, I first tackle the hallway. We quickly eliminate 30 bags of recyclables, from *House Beautiful* magazines to Sarah's Yale alumni publications and everything in between. Old stuffed toys far too damaged to be of worth and old electronics like broken cell phones and alarm clocks are deemed trash. These ladies have kept everything they have ever owned, and I have little time to sort through what amounts to an archaeological dig.

Because we have such a short time, I am aiming for big categories, like high-school memorabilia, work files, and writing projects to be stored in the attic. Normally I would take the deeper purge into those categories, knowing that sorting within a category can often be neglected, but there is no time for that. We clear the hallway and then the nursery, but every other room in the house still needs attention.

The clock runs out on us after two weeks and four six-hour sessions. Sarah e-mails to announce the birth of her son, and I can only wonder what will happen as the baby begins to need more space than the small bassinet we placed in the nursery upstairs. She promises to call back when she gets more settled into motherhood, but I know all too well that this call may never come.

THE WAY
Family influences our habits and opinions about possessions more than we realize. Understanding what our grandparents and parents pass down informs our decisions about how we interact with the material world. Once these patterns are recognized, it is up to the individual to break or maintain the cycle.

DAILY PRACTICES

✓ Clutter is a common condition that most people can fall victim to. If the situation becomes chronic and you suspect hoarding disease, consult first with a psychologist, not a professional organizer.

✓ Understand the root of your cluttering habits by reviewing your childhood home and your parent's habits. Are you part of a cycle of conspicuous cluttering, or are you breaking the mold? Compare your surroundings to those of your childhood home; it is a good barometer of how far you have come or still need to go.

✓ Assess what has been passed down to you from family members, and eliminate the guilt associated with keeping these items. If you are holding on to too much from the past, reduce your possessions to a treasured few. When we are pressured to keep things based solely on guilt, our homes and our minds become dumping grounds for items that may not hold meaning. You have the power over your possessions, not vice versa.

✓ Choose the keepsakes that hold meaning for you, not for someone else, and display them prominently. View family collectibles through the lens of what is worth passing down to the next generation. Just because something is old does not necessarily mean it is an antique or even valuable.

✓ Be careful not to assign too much meaning to memorabilia. Looking through rose-colored emotional glasses on items from our past creates a "keep it all" mentality. Be mindful of the impact of keeping too much old stuff and how it changes the way you view the future.

✓ Where children's items are concerned, old is not necessarily better. This is an area where modern ingenuity is far better than the older version.

Portion Control for Life

THE RECOMMENDED PORTION of chicken is a serving the size of a deck of cards. A big grab bag of potato chips has two portions in it. Ben & Jerry's ice cream pints serve four. This cannot be right; personally, I can eat two pieces of chicken, the entire big bag of chips, and if the ice cream flavor is S'mores, the entire pint. Is it just me who needs to re-educate myself on how much one portion is?

About 10 years ago, my misguided notion of portion size put my metabolism on the slow track to weight gain. I enlisted my brother for help, asking if he thought I should try Weight Watchers. I expected him to say no, but instead he offered to join with me. We began logging our point intake, fiber intake, and activity level, a process that took some getting used to but soon became part of our daily routine.

These are all basic tenets of any diet plan. My good friend and fellow Weight Watchers alum, Allan, put it all into perspective for me with a funny story about a meeting he attended. A fellow dieter was fixated on nectarines, specifically the amount of points in one luscious fruit. "So if a nectarine is two points, does that mean I can have three or four as long as I stay within my points?" she asked. While this seemed like a fairly innocuous question, to Allan it represented a flaw in the thinking entirely. His remark, which was met with a mix of shock and laughter, was, "Lady, none of us are here because we ate too many nectarines!" Point well taken.

I thought of this as my brother and I navigated the intricate system of counting points, logging activity points,

and recognizing the core points plan. My math skills were improving as my hunger pangs subsided. As with all diets, there were cheat days — or in our case cheat weekends. We did not follow the rules on Saturday or Sunday, which reminded me of that much-argued topic among Catholics during Lent as to whether you can eat the Snickers Bars you gave up for Lent on Sunday. (There is still too much controversy on that issue to understand the right thing to do.) But for us, on weekends we would simply put a line through the journal page when we exceeded the daily

> **With temptations abounding, resetting your meter for proper portions is essential because, like a culinary Mount Everest, you will eat it if is there.**

allotment of points. A bad day was when you had used up all of your points before lunchtime. But even so, the pounds melted away with effort and retraining, despite our weekend escapades. My portion control was starting to creep into my line-through-the-page days, as well, where too much indulging was also losing its appeal. Soon portion control was taking control of *every* aspect of my life.

"No, I don't need that J. Crew tank in every color."

"No, thanks, one Cosmopolitan is my limit!"

"No, I don't need additional batteries for the Baby Einstein Farm."

No was empowering! I was in the driver's seat, making my own choices and choosing to maintain my good habits. No longer did I feel the need to take something simply because

it was there. And any dieter can attest to the temptation of an ice cream–filled freezer or the cookie-packed cupboard. With temptations abounding, resetting your meter for proper portions is essential because, like a culinary Mount Everest, you will eat it if it is there. The pressure is on you to calibrate your choices, take control of your temptations, and maintain your good habits, as any successful dieter does.

THE WAY
Reign in your temptations, and work daily to maintain.

DAILY PRACTICES
✓ Start now.

✓ Work every day.

✓ Don't *think* about exercise — just exercise!

✓ Say no to seconds.

✓ Plan for treats.

✓ Don't let setbacks last too long.